4 Habits for Inner Peace

4 Habits for Inner Peace

By

Elizabeth A. Cronkhite

ISBN 978-1-257-76950-6

Other Books by Liz Cronkhite

The ACIM Mentor Articles: Answers for Students of *A Course in Miracles*

The Plain Language A Course in Miracles, in two books:

> *Volume One: The Message of A Course in Miracles: A translation of the Text in Plain Language*

> *Volumes Two and Three: Practicing A Course in Miracles: A translation of the Workbook in Plain Language and The Way of A Course in Miracles: A translation of the Manual for Teachers in Plain Language*

You can learn more about these books at www.acimmentor.com.

Contents

Preface

I wanted lasting peace, and there were a couple of obvious questions that came with that desire. Is lasting peace possible? And, if it is, how do I attain it?

Because peace is real and because it is within me my true desire for peace was all that was needed for the answers to come into my awareness. They came to me in 1984 in the form of *A Course in Miracles*, a self-study course for inner peace. Through the experiences to which the *Course* opened me I learned that peace is not only possible but that it is the natural state of being. I learned that I was not at peace because I was not aware of Truth. And I learned the way to be aware of Truth so as to be at peace.

I had rare glimpses of Truth before I came upon the *Course*. There were fleeting shifts within my mind of knowing that all was truly well no matter what was appearing in the world before me. Sometimes I simply knew Something Loving within me Which seemed truer than the world. I had the sense from these brief moments that if I could just get more in touch with What I experienced in them I would have everything. What the *Course* did for me was validate the Truth that I had already experienced and provide a context for me to stay in touch with It.

After twenty-two years as a student of the *Course* I started mentoring other students. By then I had attained a level of peace that could not be shaken. When students asked me how I had attained it I realized that I practiced daily four habits that I had taken from different parts of the *Course*. These were formally communing with Truth at least once a day, turning within to Truth throughout the day, calling on the Teacher of Truth within me for spiritual and practical guidance, and choosing to extend Love in my awareness to keep Love in my awareness. These habits were how I attained peace and are how I maintain peace. They are the habits that I have encouraged in other students.

The *Course* is written in a dense, lofty style that relies heavily on Christian terms and symbols that it redefines. Many struggle to understand it. So through my experiences with Truth I simplified it by writing *The Plain Language A Course in Miracles*. But afterward I found that I still longed to put down for myself in a simple, clear, and direct manner the way to peace that I have found by centering my mind in Truth. This book is the result of that desire.

In this book I call formless, limitless being *Truth* because It is the Truth and calling It what it is, is simple and direct. In other contexts I have called formless, limitless being *God*. But as it is generally used the word *God* is loaded with heavy connotations that confuse Truth and not-Truth, so I avoid it here. I elaborate on this in the section called "Truth, Not-Truth, and *God*" (Part I, 3).

I have chosen to use the term *not-Truth* instead of *illusion* when describing form because the connotation of the word *illusion* is that nothing is here. This is controversial for readers who still think of themselves as limited form rather than as limitless mind. The term *not-Truth* also states clearly what form is.

This book is appropriate for anyone who wants to find lasting peace. You may be religious or a spiritual seeker. Or you may not be religious or consider yourself spiritual at all. No matter who you are or where you come from you can use this book alone as your guide to peace or you can use it as a supplement to your study of other spiritual teachings. In any case, if you are open to It, the Truth will guide you.

Liz Cronkhite
Las Vegas, Nevada, 2011

Introduction

No one and nothing requires that you be at peace, but you could say that you insist on it. The natural state of being is boundless peace, which is an experience of wholeness and complete love and happiness. So it is inevitable that if you are not at peace you will feel the lack of it and seek for it. As Truth, peace calls to you, and its call is your own.

If you pay attention you will notice that you seek for peace all of the time in everything that you direct the personal self to do. Your desire for peace is behind every goal that you set. You believe, sometimes consciously, sometimes unconsciously. that in the next thing that you get, in the next place that you go, in the next goal that you attain, or in the next person that you meet you will find the peace that will not leave you.

And of course you do not, so you keep seeking. You may settle for less than perfect peace and accept that life in the world with its occasional bouts of contentment and transient happiness is all that there is. But settling does not provide the true peace that you seek, and you will continue to look for it. Maybe you hope that there is peace for you after the body dies. Or you may feel that the only peace is what you find in the dim imitation of true peace that you experience through overindulging in drugs, alcohol, food, sex, shopping, video or computer games, or some other obsession or addiction.

So it is never a question of whether or not you will seek for peace. The only real question is: Are you going to seek for peace where it is or continue to seek for it where you will never find it?

Inner peace is a state of mind and it results when you are aware of the Truth within you. Inner peace is an absence of conflict in your mind, so it follows that if you are not at peace you are in conflict. What is Truth and what is your conflict? These are the first questions that this book answers before elaborating on four habits that you can use to attain and maintain inner peace.

In theory you could wholly accept Truth this instant and be wholly at peace right now. But in practice attaining inner peace is a process that usually takes many years. Practicing the 4 habits for inner peace in this book will bring up your obstacles to peace much faster than if you were not consciously seeking for peace. This brings you the opportunities that you need to work through them and reach peace at an accelerated pace. This is not a comfortable process. The third section of this book discusses this so that you know what to expect, and you know which pitfalls to avoid as you center your mind in Truth to attain peace.

And finally the last section of this book uses contrasting concepts to help you sort out certain common concepts where Truth and not-Truth have become confused so that you can choose Truth and be at peace again.

I.

Truth and Not-Truth

1. Truth

Truth is formless being, which extends without limit, having no beginning and no ending. Formless being is expressed through *mind*. Its expression is knowledge of Itself because, being infinite, it is all-that-is.

There is no lack in Truth. In Truth the idea of lack does not even exist. As all-that-is formless being is an experience of wholeness, or boundless love, peace, and joy. In your seemingly-individual mind, then, your awareness of Truth brings this experience, which in this book is simply called *inner peace*.

Truth is Universal. No matter who you seem to be Truth is in your mind. You can only experience It within yourself. No words can convey It to you, though words may motivate you to open yourself to It. When you do experience Truth it is because you open your mind to It within yourself, not because It comes into your awareness from an external source.

When you touch the Truth within you, you know What It is, though you cannot define It or find an adequate label to capture It. Words and the concepts that they symbolize are too limited to capture the Limitless.

Though Truth has no beginning and no ending you may limit your awareness of It. Truth will not force its way into your awareness because It does not need your awareness to be Itself. But your awareness of It is necessary for your belief in and your experience of It. In other words, whether or not you are aware of Truth, and therefore at peace, is wholly up to you.

You do not have to earn or to attain Truth because It is always right here within you. But to be aware of Truth you do have to make the choice to be so. You can turn to It right now because it takes no time at all to be aware of Truth. But if you have obstacles (guilt, fear, feelings of unworthiness) to experiencing boundless love, peace, and joy you will have to work through them before you will allow Truth fully into your awareness. In other words, Truth takes no time to be with you because It is always here, but you may take time to become fully aware of It. Peace, then, is constant, but your experience of peace will waver until you wholly accept Truth as Truth.

You have probably had glimpses of Truth. You may have felt an unexplained peace or happiness come over you that was unrelated to anything happening in the universe of form at the time. For a moment this experience was more real and complete to you than the temporary contentment that you were used to experiencing from the world. You may have experienced a deep quiet in your mind. This experience was formless, but in it you experienced an uplifting awareness that you were in touch with all that was real. Your mind may have shifted away from the limited universe of form to an awareness of Limitlessness. Or you may have felt a Loving Presence that guided you or comforted you in a time of crisis. However it came to you, for a moment you *knew* Truth like you have never known anything in the world.

If you are not experiencing complete peace it is because you are afraid of Truth. You may have glimpses of Truth and periods of true peace, but fear is why your awareness of Truth and your experience of peace are limited. Fear may take the form of you thinking that you don't know Truth so that It seems foreign to you. You may think that you are unworthy of anything good. Or you may dismiss your experiences of Truth as "too good to be true". But these thoughts are not actually the source of your fear. They are symptoms of your attachment to not-Truth, which uses fearful thoughts to keep you unaware of Truth. Your attachment to not-Truth does not have any effect on the Truth in you, but it affects your awareness of Truth. If you want peace, then, you must be willing to look into your mind at the thoughts that are blocking your awareness of Truth.

a. Direct and Indirect Experiences of Truth

You can experience Truth in two ways: *directly* (only Truth) and *indirectly* (an effect of your awareness of Truth).

In Truth there is only Truth, and Truth knows only Truth. A *direct experience of Truth*, then, is one of knowing only Truth. This experience cannot be conveyed in words. It is an experience beyond all limitations of any kind. Truth is an experience of such wholeness that limitation, lack, and loss—therefore, the universe of limited forms including the personal self—do not exist in It, even as concepts. When you have a direct experience of Truth there is no form of any kind, no "I"; only limitless being.

A direct experience of Truth is timeless, so how long it lasts cannot be measured in time. When you return to an awareness of time from an experience of only-Truth it is likely that only a few moments will have passed no matter how long it seemed that you were "away". It will affect you profoundly. You will have seen that only the Truth is True, and you will never be able to believe in the personal self or the universe of form in the same way again. This is likely to threaten you at first. You may try to forget that it happened, but you will never be able to wholly bury the experience. In time, as you have more direct and/or indirect experiences of Truth, you will find direct experiences of Truth less frightening.

A direct experience of Truth is not something that is under your conscious personal or individual control. But it can happen only if you are ready on some level to accept the experience. Direct experiences of Truth are rare both among individual minds and within individual experiences. You can attain comprehensive peace without ever having a direct experience of Truth because when you experience Truth directly you are merely glimpsing the ultimate goal. Your mind will not stay in Truth until you are ready to wholly accept that only the Truth is True. Only-Truth is where you remain when you are wholly willing to put aside not-Truth.

An *indirect experience of Truth* is what occurs in your mind when you invite Truth into your awareness in your perception that you are a personal self in a world. It shifts your mind toward the awareness that Truth is within you and that It is the Truth. This is not the same experience as a direct experience of Truth because an indirect experience of Truth occurs while you still perceive not-Truth. Indirect experiences of Truth, then, are the bridge that you need between the perception that the world is real and the awareness that only the Truth is True. Ultimately indirect experiences of Truth prepare you to accept only-Truth by showing you, again and again, that the Truth is True. Over time indirect experiences of Truth make you aware of the Reality of Truth and the unreality of not-Truth.

Indirect experiences of Truth manifest as inner peace; an insight that shifts you toward peace or understanding Truth; a sudden knowing that the Truth is true without your leaving the awareness of the world; a sudden, uplifting, joyful awareness that all is well despite what is appearing before the body's eyes; an answer or guidance from the Teacher of Truth (your True thought system) within you; a spontaneous healing of your emotions, the body, or discord in your perception; an experience of True Love.

It is important for you to make a distinction between these two experiences. An indirect experience of Truth shows you that the Truth is within you while you still perceive not-Truth. But it is not Truth in itself. If you do not understand this distinction you could end up spiritualizing the personal experience and the universe of form. This will confuse Truth with not-Truth in your mind. Only by sorting out Truth from not-Truth can you be free to choose peace.

2. Not-Truth

Not-Truth is the exact opposite of Truth. It is time-bound, limited, and diverse form. Your experience as an individual mind in a body in a universe of form surrounded by a multiplicity of other limited minds and forms is not-Truth.

Certainly it seems to you as though all of this exists and is real, and this perception is the source of your conflict. There is only One Reality and It is Truth. But you live in the perception of two opposed realities in one of two ways. You deny Truth and believe that only your personal experience is reality. Or you think that your personal experience is equally as real as Truth.

You can never wholly undo Truth in your mind, but you can choose to be unaware of It. This denial buries the conflict in your mind, but it does not undo it. Truth persists in your mind whether or not you are aware of It. On some level you know this. And Truth being the Truth you naturally long for It just as you do for the wholeness, peace, and joy that are the natural effect of being aware of Truth.

Being aware of Truth while still holding onto not-Truth as reality also does not undo your conflict. It just brings your conflict out into the open. You may think that there is no conflict here. But both Truth and not-Truth cannot co-exist in your mind since they are diametrically opposed. Not-Truth denies Truth and Truth undoes not-Truth. You cannot combine them, but you are likely to attempt this when you first become aware of Truth.

When you first become aware of Truth not-Truth is still more real to you than Truth. So you think that the value of Truth is in how It can inform your personal, or not-True, experience. You may attempt to "spiritualize" not-Truth by trying to conform not-Truth to Truth. For example, you may adopt politics that you think reflect the love or oneness that you experienced in Truth. Or you may try to form a code of conduct, morality, or ethics based on your experiences of Truth. But any time that you try to force your personal experience or the world into a mold that you think reflects Truth you will lose sight of Truth. Truth has nothing at all to do with not-Truth. The value of Truth is in Itself. Its value to you is in the peace that comes to you when you are aware of It as Reality. By trying to mold not-Truth to Truth you confuse them in your mind and perpetuate your sense of conflict.

a. The Origin and Perpetuation of Not-Truth

To understand the conflict in your mind it is important that you understand how wholly dependent not-Truth is on Truth or, more correctly, on the denial of Truth.

Truth is all-that-is so there is nothing that can exist beside It. But being all-that-is It contains the idea of Its Own opposite. However, the nature of All undoes the idea of Its Own opposite the moment that the idea arises. But Truth is eternal, or timeless, so the idea of Its seeming-opposite contains *time*. In the idea of time, then, It seems as though not-Truth began long ago and will be undone in some indefinite future. In Eternity, however, the idea of not-Truth is over the instant that it arises. Not-Truth does not exist at all.

So limited-form-as-reality, or not-Truth, is only perpetuated in your mind through your perception that time and all that it contains is real. Not-Truth has billions of time-bound stories within greater stories of time to "prove" its existence. For example, one of the greater stories is that not-Truth began 14 billion years ago in a "big bang". This put the universe of form into motion and eventually evolved into the universe of form that you perceive today. As a person, you see your story as a part of this universe of form. Another story is that ten thousand years ago the universe of form was made by a god in seven days and seven nights. This god eventually peopled the world, set them up to defy him, and when they did punished them and all who came after.

In the world there are thousands of origin stories for the universe of form. Whichever "macro" story of time that you choose for not-Truth you have your own "micro" time-bound story within it. You seem to be born into this greater story to make your own story. You spend this "life" defining and defending this story. But really on a seemingly-individual mind level this story that you have for a personal self merely perpetuates not-Truth in your mind. It seems real but is actually an idea that is already undone. You cannot know this, however, until you choose to turn inward and experience the timelessness of Truth right now. Only now in this instant within your mind can you step out of time and experience the Truth.

There is no intention that brings not-Truth into seeming-existence. It is only an idea that can never be real, so it has no purpose at all. Just as Truth simply is the idea of not-Truth simply is, too. But what it is, is only an idea. However, within the idea of not-Truth, not-Truth does have the intention of undoing Truth. So when you believe its thoughts you experience its intentions as real and harmful. But though this experience seems very real to you it has no effect at all on the Truth in you. In Truth it is harmless.

You can liken your mind when it is caught up in not-Truth to being like a child sleeping warm and safe in a loving parent's arms while having a nightmare. While the terrible dream seems real enough to the child while they are having it, in reality the child is safe and warm and loved. So, just as the child can awaken from the nightmare you can choose to withdraw your mind from the world of form and turn it inward to Truth and peace.

As long as you listen to and follow the thought system of not-Truth in your mind you will not experience the peace and happiness that are the natural state of being. This is not because you are "bad" or doing something "wrong", but because you are simply not in touch with the Truth within you.

b. Your Seemingly-Individual Mind

Truth is Timeless, so not-Truth is time. Truth is Formless, so not-Truth is form. Truth is Limitless, so not-Truth is limited. Truth is one—singular and the same throughout Itself—so not-Truth is a diverse multiplicity. Truth is peace, so not-Truth is conflict.

The universe of form, then, is the opposite of Truth. It is a projection of the idea of not-Truth in the part of Mind where the idea of not-Truth seems to occur. Being the opposite of Oneness and Formlessness it seems to manifest diversity of form. This includes bodies onto which it projects replicas of its own split mind. What you think of as your individual mind, then, is a projection of the moment in the Mind of Truth of *the idea of not-Truth/the undoing-of-the-idea-of-not-Truth*. So beyond not-Truth in your seemingly-individual mind Truth resides. While not-Truth in your mind seems to take the form of a unique mind and "personality", the Truth in your mind is universal and is the only part of your mind that is real.

You seem to have two thought systems in your mind, then. One comes from Truth and the other is the idea of not-Truth in the form of a *personal thought system*. Your True thought system leads you inward to an awareness of the Truth within you. The personal thought system in your mind is engaged wholly in perpetuating your belief in not-Truth as reality. Your True thought system is the natural effect of your awareness of Truth. It only requires your openness to Truth to come into your awareness. The personal thought system, however, being unreal, requires your active attention to continue in your awareness.

You seem to be an individual mind that was born into a body in a world. But really you are a mind identifying with the idea of a body in a world. Your mind is a projection of the part of Mind which seems to be split between Truth and not-Truth. So you have a choice as to which thought system in your mind to follow. This choice is determined solely by your goal for yourself. If you want lasting peace you must learn to let go of your attachment to not-Truth and to hold only Truth in your mind. If you make this choice then you become Truth reawakening to Itself. If, however, identifying with a personal self is more important to you than peace you will continue in the perception of a world of limitation, conflict, and loss as reality. You will not have lasting peace. You may make the choice to allow Truth into your awareness on a limited basis, which will result in brief moments of peace, but not in lasting peace.

Whichever choice you make it has no effect on Truth. Truth continues untouched by the idea of not-Truth, which has never really occurred. Only within the idea of not-Truth does not-Truth seem to be occurring. The conflict between Truth and not-Truth, then, is wholly within your mind. So the choice between lasting peace and lack of peace is also wholly within your mind.

c. Your Obstacles to Inner Peace: Guilt/Fear, Attachment, and Projection

Both Truth and not-Truth perpetuate themselves. Truth does this simply by being What It is: limitless. Not-Truth, however, cannot simply be because it does not exist at all. It requires your belief in it for it to seem to exist for you. When you do believe in it, it uses its built-in self-perpetuating ideas to hold your attention. These are guilt and fear, your belief that it has something to offer you, and the projection of its traits onto Truth.

Your True thought system inspires only peace in you. The personal thought system inspires only fear in some form in you. Both thought systems are benign. Your True thought system is benign because It is one, which is another way to say that It is wholly loving. The personal thought system is benign because it is not real. However, as long as you believe in it you will not experience it as benign. It does have the intention of undoing the Truth in your mind.

Truth cannot be undone, but the idea of it being undone is frightening to you. If you believe that the personal self is you then you believe that you have undone Truth. You feel guilty, and you live in a state of fear. You think that you have attacked Truth, and projecting your own thoughts you expect that Truth is going to attack you back. You cannot escape guilt and fear when you identify with a personal self because to believe that you are a personal self you must believe that you have undone Truth.

Truth, of course, is oblivious to this attack that has never happened. But when you identify as a personal self you believe, unconsciously, that you are guilty and deserve to be attacked back. This belief is manifest in the countless ways that guilt seems real to you in the universe of form. It is expressed most obviously through not-Truth's various religions, which emphasize "sin". The belief that you have attacked Truth is the underlying source of all of your guilt and fear no matter what you think the source of your guilt and fear may be.

For example, perhaps in your identification with a personal self you did something to someone that you have judged as harmful to them.You feel guilty for this. You would not even have this specific story for guilt if you did not believe that you were a personal self. This identification is the true origin of your guilt and fear. The guilt and fear that manifest in specific instances of the personal self's story are simply representations of your belief that you attacked Truth and that guilt and fear are justified for this.

Any judgment of guilt or fear on manifestations in the universe of form are projections of the guilt and fear that you believe are justified in your own mind. It does not matter where you see guilt and fear as real. If you see them as real anywhere you believe that they are real for you.

Since not-Truth can never be real there is never any justification for guilt and fear. But in your belief that guilt is justified you will punish yourself. You will do this either because you believe right out that you deserve it or because you hope that doing so will mitigate the punishment that you expect from Truth. Your punishment may take the form of you actually doing something you deem harmful to yourself, like losing or destroying something important to you. Or it may come in the form of you interpreting a generic, impersonal event, such as a natural disaster, as being your punishment.

Guilt and fear are also the shield that the personal thought system uses to keep you from looking inward to Truth. It tells you, sometimes unconsciously, sometimes quite overtly, to not look within your own mind because you will find out how truly "bad" you are.

When you identify with a personal self, then, you always feel that you deserve punishment and you never feel that you deserve "good". You are always insecure and vulnerable. You never feel that you have paid enough, up front or afterward, for what you have "done wrong" or for the "good" that has come to you. You may cover up this sense of inadequacy by going to the other extreme and exaggerating your self-worth. But this will only mask your guilt and fear. It will not undo them.

The guilt and fear of the personal thought system can never be removed from it Nor can it be corrected from within it because guilt and fear are its very fabric. This is why you can never be wholly at peace while you remain attached to the personal thought system. The only way to release yourself from the cycle of guilt-fear and the punishment that they motivate you to bring upon yourself, then, is to release the personal thought system and identify with Truth.

While the personal thought system uses guilt and fear to keep you attached to it and away from Truth you are also attached to a personal identity for its own sake. You believe that it and its world have value for you and that they offer you something that Truth does not offer. In fact, you are engaged in trying to find this elusive, non-existent something the whole time that you are identified with a personal self. This is how the personal thought system works to maintain itself in your awareness. It lies to you about Truth by telling you that Truth will punish you while it promises you that you will find something greater than Truth if you follow it instead. Of course you cannot find anything greater than everything. The personal thought system's empty promise only holds sway over you as long as you do not experience Truth. Once you experience Truth you know that It is everything and you begin to question the value of not-Truth. You will vacillate between Truth and the personal thought system's mesmerizing but undeliverable promises for a while. But you will never wholly believe the personal thought system again.

Finally, another obstacle to inner peace is the personal thought system's projections of itself onto Truth. It is because you confuse Truth with not-Truth that you fear Truth. For example, because not-Truth is full of empty promises you find it hard to believe Truth's promise of lasting love, peace, and joy. You think that what Truth offers you is "too good to be true" because in the world of not-Truth what seems too good to be true always is. Any time that you find it hard to trust Truth it is because you are projecting an attribute of not-Truth onto It. This is why to be at peace it is so essential that you sort out Truth from not-Truth. (There is more on this in the next part, *Truth, Not-Truth, and* God).

d. Not-Truth and Time

Since Truth is timeless not-Truth uses the idea of time to play out its seeming-reality. In your seemingly-individual mind this means that the personal thought system uses the idea of time to give the personal self a "story" or seeming existence. It may also use concepts like *preordination* and *reincarnation* to make it seem as though the personal self can exist beyond the idea of time. But neither time nor the personal self exist at all. Both are just ideas in your mind right now.

As was stated earlier your mind is the moment of *the idea of the-opposite-of-Truth/the undoing of the idea of the-opposite-of-Truth.* In the present within you, you are always in Timelessness. But you can think that you are in time. So the way out of time is to turn your mind away from ideas of time by bringing your mind into the present and turning it inward to Truth. Every instant, then, your choice is to point your mind outward to the story of time and its universe of form or inward to Truth. Your choice is determined by whether you want conflict or peace.

Not-Truth emphasizes the past and the future because they are never here. Truth emphasizes the present because It is always here. Only at this moment can you turn inward to Truth and experience peace.

Look honestly at the ideas of past and future:

You can and do have any story that the personal thought system wants you to have about the past. In your identification with a personal self you even change your mind about the past as you "learn more" about it. So it is clearly not True. For something to be True it must always be True or sometimes it would be not True. Truth cannot be not-Truth and still be Truth.

The past is a story about which many personal selves may agree to some degree, but about which no two personal selves are ever wholly in agreement. For each the past is just a personalized story with some collective elements. Clearly, there is no objective past at all.

The future never arrives so any thoughts that you have about the future are pure fantasy. These fantasies are based on what you seemed to learn in your story for the past. The personal thought system, then, projects into the future from the story that it has for your past.

Your whole identification with a personal self is based on a past story. The resentments and guilt that you hold in your mind are all from past stories. If those stories were real they could not be undone because they would be past and not here. This is why you cannot undo resentment and guilt through the personal thought system. It uses the idea of time to make it seem that your resentments and guilt cannot be undone because their sources are not here. They are in the past. But really if you are experiencing resentment and guilt now their sources must be thoughts in your mind now. So the way out of resentment and guilt is to find the thoughts in your mind now that are causing you to feel resentment and guilt. Then you can release them and come into the present with Truth.

Memories from the past and fantasies for the future are obstacles to peace because you are not present to Truth when you are caught up in them. Your choice to be aware of Truth or not is a choice that you make now. So no thought about the past or fantasy for the future has to have any effect on your peace now.

The personal thought system uses time to keep you from Truth and peace. You cannot be with Truth in the past because the past is not here. You cannot be with Truth in the future because the future never arrives. If you watch the personal thought system's thoughts you will notice that they are all about the past, a possible future (projected from the past), or simply "someplace else". The personal thought system's thoughts are never in the present when you can turn inward and find Truth and peace.

3. Truth, Not-Truth, and *God*

Truth, being all that is, has no questions. But not-Truth, being nothing at all, is full of them. Its central question is "What am I?" This question is at the heart of the personal thought system. Throughout its seeming-life the personal self seeks to make itself real by defining, defending, and validating itself, and one of its most essential questions is the nature of its origin.

Whether or not you have chosen a religious or a scientific explanation to explain the origins of the personal self with which you identify you must be aware of concepts of a *Creator* or *God*. You may be wondering if What is called *Truth* in this book is the same as *God*. This is a valid and important question. The concept that is generally thought of as *God* is usually accepted or rejected out of fear. If you equate What is termed *Truth* in this book with the generally accepted concept of *God* this fear will keep you from opening your mind to an awareness of Truth. And if you are not open to Truth you will not experience peace.

As the word *Truth* is used in this book it refers to formless being. Truth has no beginning and no ending. The experience of It is boundless love, peace, and joy. Like the word *Truth* the word *God* is a symbol. It can stand for whatever you want it to mean. But as it is generally used the word *God* refers to the maker of the universe of form. In some origin stories one is to view the mind in its identification with a personal self as being made in the image of the mind of God. In other origin stories one is to view the personal mind and the body as made in the image of God's mind and body. So in either of these cases *God* refers to what in this book is called *not-Truth*. It has no reality. It is only a construct of your mind.

The universe of form, including personal thought systems, is a projection of not-Truth. So you can say that the personal self and its body are "made in the image of" not-Truth. But the personal thought system is only an erroneous aspect of your seemingly-split mind. It is not all that is in your mind. Truth is also in your mind. So you have probably also experienced Truth, and chances are that some of those experiences you have labeled *God* as well. In fact the term *God* is loaded with connotations for both Truth and not-Truth. This is because a split mind always projects its conflict onto its concept of its origin. In other words, you are not "made in God's image" but the commonly held concept of God is made in the image of your split mind.

Oneness is the natural state of Mind. Even the part of Mind that thinks that it is split between Truth and not-Truth seeks desperately for the Unity that its seeming-split negates. But since Truth cannot be undone in Mind the only way to have unity and still maintain not-Truth is to reconcile Truth and not-Truth. This cannot happen of course because each would undo the other. If Truth has any element of not-Truth It is not True. And not-Truth can never be Truth. This conflict is reflected in the chaotic world that the split mind projects. This conflict is also in your seemingly-individual mind. It is the source of your lack of peace.

In your individual mind, then, you have two gods, Truth and not-Truth. Your concepts of each are so entwined with the other that you see them as one and the same. You experience both and project the attributes of each onto the other. Then you project this jumbled-up god outside of you so that it seems that it created you rather than that you made it up. It is essential for you to look at this and that you sort out Truth and not-Truth. If you equate this contradictory and arbitrary god with Truth you will inevitably fear Truth and not invite It into your awareness. Then you will not be able to choose peace.

As an example of how your mind tries to fuse Truth and not-Truth look at two common, contradictory concepts of God that one usually holds at the same time: God is Love and God is the creator of the universe of form. The universe of form is a place of painful limitations, and the personal experience is one of lack and loss, even up to the death of the personal self. This is cruelty, not love. So it is clear that if God is Love then God could not have created the universe of form. Or if God made the universe of form then God must not be Love.

If you hold both of these concepts of God in your mind you may state that God is Love but you could not truly believe it. How could you? Your experience of the limited world and the personal life contradict the experience of limitlessness and wholeness that is Love. A perfect universe of form and personal experience are impossible. Each personal self has its own set of values and each projects its own meaning onto the universe of form. Further, even if each seemingly-individual mind came to understand this the personal experience would still be one of painful limitations. When you attempt to entwine Boundless Love (Truth) with lack and limitation (not-Truth) then you end up believing either that Boundless Love does not exist or that It is treacherous and untrustworthy.

Truth is Love because It is the Truth. If you use the word *God* to refer to the boundless love, peace and joy of Truth then *God* means Love. But *God* then cannot refer to the maker of the universe of form. If you use the word *God* to mean both Love and the maker of the universe of form then *God* means an arbitrary, contradictory being that rightfully should be feared. So if you intend to use the word *God* to mean what is meant by Truth in this book then you must make sure that you have the definition of God-as-Truth clear in your mind. Otherwise you will fall back into thinking of *God* as something to be feared. Then you will not welcome Truth and the peace that It inspires into your awareness.

a. Righteousness or Peace

Peace is your True state of being so not-Truth has no investment in your attaining inner peace. But while you are not at peace you are compelled to seek for it. So the personal thought system in your mind must do something with this desire. It is perfectly content to lead you on a search for peace, but it can never lead you to actually finding it. Only your True thought system can do that because truly finding peace means releasing the personal thought system.

The personal thought system offers you many means for seeking for peace through the personal self. For example, in others, by attaining certain material objects, by reaching certain goals, in idealized situations, etc. It also tells you that peace will come to you when the personal self is *right*.

Being right means the personal self behaving correctly in the eyes of family, culture, a god, a religious institution, or according to a moral code or philosophy. It can also mean its being in with the *right group* of people or simply being the winner in an argument or contest. (Might makes right). But which behavior, group, or side in an argument or contest is designated as *right* varies between individuals, cultures, religions, philosophies, and over time. Since there is no objective *right* this leads to conflicts within and among individuals and between cultures, religions, etc. So obviously righteousness leads to further conflict, not to peace. The personal thought system's remedies for this are righteous indignation, compulsive perfectionism, and the promise of a reward for righteous behavior after the personal self dies. None of these bring you peace, but they do keep you seeking for it in the next "right way".

Your lack of peace is not of concern to the personal thought system. It is only concerned with maintaining itself in your mind. It uses your desire for peace, then, for its own purpose. Only bodies behave. As long as your mind is occupied with behavior, yours or others', you maintain your identification with a body. And while you are consumed with constantly judging behavior, yours or others', guilt stays in the forefront of your mind. If there is "right" behavior there is also "wrong" behavior.

As form, the body and the personal thought system are thoughts in your mind. The body's behavior, then, follows from thought. The mind may think about behavior, but behavior does not cause the thoughts about it. What you think about behavior is a choice that you make in the mind.

Since inner peace comes only from an awareness of Truth the concept of right behavior is irrelevant to attaining inner peace. The only appropriate question about behavior in relation to inner peace is, which behavior is helpful for attaining and maintaining inner peace? When you choose inner peace the behavior that is conducive to attaining it will happen automatically because behavior is an effect of thought. For example, you chose inner peace in your mind then you directed the body to find a book about attaining inner peace.

It never makes sense to judge behavior because the body's behavior can look the same when your mind is centered in Truth as when it is occupied with the personal thought system. When you choose inner peace your overall life becomes simpler, slower, and quieter. But the day to day motions of the body in your awareness do not vary greatly from before you chose peace. It still eats, sleeps, goes to work, enjoys its friends and family, watches television, goes golfing, celebrates holidays, etc. Inner peace is a state of mind, not of behavior. If you change your behavior to appear more "spiritual" you are spiritualizing not-Truth. This means that you are trying to make not-Truth perfect, like Truth. This makes the personal thought system tell you that you are righteous, but it has nothing to do with inner peace.

If you want inner peace, then, the question is never which behavior, group, or side is right. It is, do you want to pursue directing the personal self to be right or do you want to be at peace? You cannot have it both ways because pursuing right behavior is an obstacle to peace. Peace comes only from an awareness of Truth.

4. Sorting Out Truth and Not-Truth

It may seem particularly difficult for you to understand how all that you perceive with the body's eyes and think about with the personal thought system is not real. But think about this: For something to be True it must always be True. Otherwise It would sometimes be not True. Truth cannot sometimes be not True and still be Truth. That Truth is always the same is what makes It Truth. Truth is the constant on which you can rely.

The only constant in not-Truth, however, is change. Everything in the universe of form changes, even mountains and planets and stars. The personal self and the body with which you identify change constantly. It may take a second or minutes or years or millennia or eons for the changes to occur, but nothing is static in not-Truth.

When you realize that everything that you have thought was true is not True it is frightening. But the Truth is within you and It can never change. It has not changed because you thought that not-Truth is real. It is not changed by anything that does or does not seem to happen in the universe of form. Nothing that you think or say or do as a personal self can change It. Eternal Love is unwavering within you. This is why if you want inner peace the only change that has any real value for you is to become aware of Truth. You can find peace only in the Constant.

a. Truth, Not-Truth, and the Law of Mind

If you choose lasting peace the way must begin by you sorting out the two thought systems in your mind. Both seem real to you and both have been ascribed the attributes of the other. Only when you see clearly how both thought systems work can you make the choice for Truth and peace.

You have only one mind and it works the same throughout. But the two thought systems in it each use the Law of Mind differently. The Law of Mind is that *mind knows only itself.* This means that mind is really only aware of what is in itself. It is always only looking inward. But where your True thought system acknowledges this the personal thought system does not.

Your True thought system looks inward at Truth and knows that It is real. So it extends in your awareness the wholeness and peace and happiness that it sees within. For example, let's say that you are driving past a messy car accident. If your mind is turned inward to Truth you will be at peace. Your experience of love will extend to your perception of the accident. This may take the form of you recognizing that the accident is only an appearance. The reality of the love in your mind beyond the perception of the accident will be more real to you.

If there is action to take you will know how to direct the body. Any action will be effortless because it will be Love moving through you. If there is no action to take you will look away, your peace untouched.

Your True thought system recognizes that your experience of peace or conflict is determined by which thought system you choose. It is not determined by what seems to be appearing. It can acknowledge this because it is True. Being True It has nothing to hide.

The personal thought system, however, also looks inward. But then it projects what is in it outward and denies that the meaning that it sees comes from within. Using the example of the car accident, if your mind is turned inward to the personal thought system you will experience fear and horror as you look on the accident as you project your thoughts onto it. You will blame the accident for your feelings of vulnerability, for the memories of past injuries that you've experienced, for the people that you have lost in accidents, or for whatever painful and fearful thoughts that the accident seems to evoke.

The actual origin of your feelings of vulnerability, pain, and loss will be your identification with a personal self in a body in a world that is dangerous to personal selves and bodies. To maintain your belief that its thoughts represent reality the personal thought system requires that you project them away. Your thoughts then seem to be happening to you. The personal thought system is one of self-deception. Being not-True it must operate in denial. Otherwise you would see that it has no foundation and let it go.

Though it is a projection of not-Truth and the opposite of Truth in every way the universe of form is in itself without meaning. When you look on the world from your True thought system you recognize that it is only an appearance. Your inner awareness of peace, love, and joy as reality are untouched by it. As you seem to move about the world you carry this awareness with you everywhere you go. You rest within in peace, no matter what is appearing.

But the personal thought system sees meaning in everything in the world. It projects that meaning itself then denies this. It teaches you that what you think about the world is fact. You then cannot see that the universe of form is neutral and meaningless. You respond to your thoughts about the world as though they are not your thoughts but something happening to you. You feel powerless, helpless, and afraid. Your conflict is magnified because each seemingly-individual mind around you also projects its own meaning onto the world. Everyone insists that what they see is fact or at least the "right way" to look at the world. In not-Truth everyone does "live in their own little world".

So the first step on your way back to peace is to recognize that you have two opposed thought systems in your mind. You must learn to observe how they both work. Only after you have sorted each from the other will you see a clear choice between them. One will hold you in conflict and the other will lead you to peace.

b. Knowing instead of Thinking

The Being and the Mind of Truth are one and the same. Truth *knows* only Truth. When you experience Truth you know Truth. This is the same as saying that you are Truth. So knowing Truth and being Truth are one and the same experience.

Not-Truth is the *idea* of the opposite of Truth. It has no being or real existence. It has no mind to know anything. In your mind it is a system of thoughts. So you can *think* about not-Truth but never *know* it. It is through your thoughts about it and its universe of form that it seems real to you.

The distinction between knowing Truth and thinking about not-Truth is important for you in sorting out the opposed experiences of not-Truth and Truth. When you experience Truth directly you know It. Your recognition that It is Reality surpasses any personal experience of "knowing". In Truth you have no questions and nothing about which to think. Truth is a subtle, natural, effortless, and profound experience of being.

But when you choose to experience not-Truth you expend a lot of effort in the form of *thought*. You are probably not even aware of how much effort you put into holding not-Truth in your mind. This is because you want it so you are willing to make the effort. But as you observe your mind and you experience the effortless, subtle Presence of Truth in it you will come to see that your belief in not-Truth does not happen of itself. Not-Truth requires your active effort to seem to exist for you at all.

You may think that both Truth and not-Truth are real because your awareness vacillates between both. Both experiences can certainly seem real to you. But when you look upon your experiences of not-Truth from an awareness of Truth their unreality is obvious to you. They are undone for you. In contrast, when you think that you are aware of not-Truth you may deny Truth, but this only hides Truth from your awareness. It does not undo Truth.

Your True thought system is the Teacher of Truth in your mind. It is a bridge between Truth and not-Truth. Truth is not threatened by not-Truth because not-Truth does not exist. So when you turn to the Teacher of Truth in your mind It leads you to look on not-Truth from an awareness that the Truth is True. Then you see that not-Truth is not True. This is how not-Truth is undone in your mind.

But the ideas in not-Truth will never lead you to look on Truth. Not-Truth disappears in the Presence of Truth. When you empower its thought system in your mind it will block Truth from your awareness. But it cannot undo Truth in your mind because Truth is your mind's Reality. It will distract you from Truth with its thoughts about a personal self and a world. It will put up guilt as an obstacle to your awareness of Truth. And it will teach you to fear Truth so that you will not look within for Truth. None of this, however, makes not-Truth any more than a collection of ideas.

Thinking is your split mind's substitute for knowing. But give thinking to the Teacher of Truth in your mind and it will use it to lead you back to knowing. When you listen to the Teacher of Truth you have a sense of joyous liberation from limitations and fear. You know that you are listening to the personal thought system when you feel guilty or afraid.

It is essential for you to understand that intellectually understanding a spiritual teaching is not the same as experiencing or knowing Truth. Thoughts in your mind, written, spoken, or conveyed in any form are never Truth. They can only point you toward Truth when you see or hear them through the Teacher of Truth in your mind. Thoughts inspired by a direct or indirect experience of Truth will comfort and guide you. But it is the experience of Truth, not the thoughts themselves, that shifts you toward peace.

There are many ideas that you will need to examine to sort out Truth and not-Truth in your mind. Some of these are explored in Part IV of this book. But now that the reason for your lack of peace—you are unaware of Truth—has been made clear it is time for you to move past theory and into practice. This practice will bring Truth into your awareness and lead you to lasting inner peace.

II.

4 Habits for Inner Peace

Introduction

Inner peace is the result of knowing that only the Truth is True. You cannot sort out the True and the un-True thought systems in your mind until you consciously experience Truth. Otherwise only not-Truth will seem real to you and Truth will be just a nice idea. Also, you cannot recognize that not-Truth is not True from its thought system. You can only recognize this when you look on it from the awareness that the Truth is True.

You do not attain Truth because It is always within you. But you attain peace by becoming aware of Truth and by keeping It in your awareness. This section discusses four habits that you can incorporate into your life to attain and maintain an awareness of Truth. Therefore they can lead you to attain and maintain an experience of peace.

The great advantage to you in practicing these four habits is that they undo your greatest obstacles to peace: Your unconscious belief that you are guilty for attacking and undoing Truth and your fear that Truth will punish you for this. This belief is at the very core of the personal identity. It functions as a defense to perpetuate the personal thought system in your mind. Do not underestimate your belief that this is true because it is the primary reason that you fear Truth and you are not at peace. But by allowing Truth into your awareness again you are showing yourself that what the personal thought system tells you is a lie. Your experiencing Truth even once is enough to show you that Truth is still within you, untouched. This undoes the personal thought system's entire premise for guilt and fear.

Practicing these four habits will accelerate your awareness of all of your obstacles to peace. As was discussed in the first part of this book, besides guilt your obstacles to peace are your desire for and attachment to not-Truth and your projections of not-Truth onto Truth. Each of these obstacles takes the form of thoughts in your mind. You will naturally bump into these thoughts as you attempt to bring and hold Truth in your awareness. Bringing them up from your subconscious and undoing them is the process necessary for you to be wholly at peace.

How you integrate these habits into your life depends on what works best for you. You may want to take several weeks to integrate one habit into your life before adding another and doing the same until all four are daily habits.

Or if you already have some experience with one or more of these you may want to begin them all at once. Just make sure that you do not overwhelm yourself or you will lose your motivation to practice any of them.

1. Habit #1: Commune with Truth Daily

"I quiet my mind and open it to Truth."

Truth is with you always, so you only have to invite It into your conscious awareness for It to come into your conscious awareness. Doing this alone on a daily basis will be enough to transform your mind and your experience toward peace. In fact, this habit alone will lead to the other habits because the rewards of being aware of Truth will motivate you to keep It in your awareness.

Very simply, this habit is sitting quietly and comfortably where you will not be disturbed, turning your mind inward with your eyes opened or closed, and inviting Truth to come into your mind. There are three experiences that you will have when you sit down to meditate:

a. Processing

Processing refers to what occurs in your mind any time that you still the activity of the body or keep it busy with rote activity. The mind begins to go over what has happened that day, to mull over perceived problems, to analyze a book that you've read or a movie that you've watched, etc. Especially if you have just experienced or you anticipate experiencing anything that you judge as emotionally significant your mind will be full of it. This processing can take many minutes to wind down. Do not engage with these thoughts or fight against them. Simply let them come up and go by. Both engaging with them and fighting them will make these thoughts more real to you. If you find your mind engaging with a thought simply stop and let it go. Gently remind yourself that this is your time for quieting your mind and opening it to Truth.

If, however, you find that you have a great deal to process you may need to separate your processing time from your communing time. Allow yourself to have a processing meditation then have another communing meditation later in the day when your mind is quieter and you are more willing to open to Truth.

This observing-without-getting-involved is an important part of training your mind to be aware of Truth as you seem to be in a world. The personal thought system will prattle on with its story for you and its world until you let go of the personal thought system entirely. So you must learn how to let it run while you return your attention again and again to Truth. Just as you know that the sun is still there when clouds pass before it you can be aware of the Truth as personal thoughts pass by. This practice during meditation will eventually extend into the rest of your life. You will find yourself resting in peace as you let whatever is appearing in the universe of form pass before you.

Another essential benefit of this practice is that as you step back and observe the personal thought system you learn that it is not you. The mere fact that you can observe it teaches this to you. If the personal thought system was you, you would not be able to detach from it and watch it. This practice is the beginning of your awareness that you have two entirely different thought systems in your mind. Only one represents the Truth in you.

b. Meditating with the Teacher of Truth in Your Mind

Your True thought system is not Truth in Its entirety. But it is the Part of your mind that still knows Truth while you think that you are a personal self in a world. It functions as a bridge in your mind between Truth and your perception that not-Truth is real. At first It will seem new to you. It will seem like it is "other" than you because It is so unlike the personal thought system to which you are used to listening. You can think of It, then, as the *Teacher of Truth* in your mind. You can build your trust in It by making It your Constant Companion in your perception that you are in a world. This trust will eventually lead to you identifying with It. (This process is elaborated on in Habit #3).

You may have a specific question or something that you want to sort from your spiritual study, practice, or your life in general. These you want to bring this to the Teacher of Truth to use for peace. It may help you to do this when you settle down to meditate and can focus on the question or idea with the Teacher of Truth. This is an intellectual activity and it is not the same as communing with or experiencing Truth. But this practice is important for opening yourself to experience Truth, for learning to trust Truth, and for working through the thoughts that are obstacles to peace. The Teacher of Truth will always answer you, but keep in mind that you may not always hear the answers right away. You can let go of the thought or concern and trust that the answer will come when you are ready for it. Meditation can be the time when you choose to release the question or the thought to the Teacher of Truth in your mind.

When Truth responds to your questions the answer can come in the form of a still, quiet Voice in your mind, an intuition, or simply an unformed idea. Sometimes you may even hear the answer through another or through something that you read or watch on television or see in a movie. The form in which the answer comes to you and its relationship to your initial question are not relevant because the answer is really coming from within you. The answer is always immediately in your mind, but you will only recognize it when you are ready to receive it.

In time as you work through your guilt and trust the Teacher of Truth more and more you will be ready to receive answers right away. You will even be able to join in conversation with the Teacher of Truth, both during meditation and in the normal course of the day.

You may want to include meditating with the Teacher of Truth with your daily practice of communing with Truth. Or, you may want to set aside time for meditating with Truth apart from your time of communing with Truth.

c. Communing with Truth

Communing with Truth is the practice that is truly transformative for you. It means inviting Truth into your awareness and then resting in It. After you have processed and brought your questions to the Teacher of Truth let your thoughts go by as you sink deeper into the still quiet at the center of your mind. Truth is always right here within you. You do not have to reach for It or to seek for It. You just need to be with It. Don't worry about having a completely quiet mind. Just return your mind to the quiet again and again as you let go of any thoughts that come up. Know that Truth is here with you.

If you find yourself very resistant remind yourself why you are communing with Truth: "I invite Truth into my conscious awareness so that I will be at peace."

The goal here is not for you to enter into an altered state or a trance but for you to enter wholly into the present with Truth. You are not likely to feel anything dramatic. Truth is natural, so your experience of it will be subtle, though profound. If you find yourself spontaneously taking a deep breath and relaxing deeper you can be sure that you have touched Truth. Rest in It for a while longer, allowing yourself to be at peace. You can be certain that if you have truly opened your mind to Truth It has come closer to your conscious awareness.

You may find that it is not when you are meditating that you experience peace. But as you go about your day peace will come over you, often when you least expect it. Formally communing with Truth is your invitation to It to come into your awareness. However, you may not be fully ready for It to do so until another time. It is your willingness in the moment to experience Truth, not any effort that you are making, which opens your awareness to Truth. Your making the effort everyday to put aside time to commune with Truth demonstrates your overall willingness to be at peace.

Your mind's resistance to this practice will be very intense at the beginning. The personal thought system with which you are used to identifying does not want you looking inward. It is afraid that you will look past it to Truth. It will tell you that you should not look within because you will see how "bad" you really are. It may not say this openly, but you can be sure that this will be part of your initial resistance. Remember, though, that the goal is not for you to practice some sort of perfect meditation or to attain a perfectly quiet mind. The goal is to simply open your mind to Truth, no matter what else is in your mind.

Use any words or symbols or images that help you to quiet your mind and release the personal thought system's chaotic babbling. You may prefer total quiet or find that music or other sounds help you to stay present. You can also choose to learn formal meditation techniques. Over time you may have to vary your approach because what works for a while may stop working. There is no one right way to quiet your mind and commune with Truth because the form of meditation itself is not the goal.

It may take you years before you feel that you have any consistent results from a daily practice of meditation. But every sincere attempt you make to invite Truth into your awareness will cumulatively result in an experience of lasting peace.

At first set aside an hour a day to practice the habit of communing with Truth. It is best if you can do this as early in the day as possible. But if the morning is not the best time for you do it at a time when your resistance is at its lowest ebb. In time you will be able to determine how long it typically takes you to quiet your mind and open it to Truth. Then you may shorten or lengthen the time as needed. You will also learn to gauge on which days you feel committed to having a longer meditation and on which days it is best to simply make the attempt because you are not feeling very committed.

It is not helpful for you to get angry or to punish yourself when your mind is busy or because you are resistant to quieting it. Inner peace is a choice that you make for yourself because you love yourself. It is not something that is "right" or that is required by anything outside of you. If your resistance is strong and you find yourself becoming increasingly uncomfortable during a meditation stop and try again later.

The peace that comes to you from communing with Truth every day will often be hard for you to explain, even to yourself. You will find yourself more content and your mind quieter even when it seems that nothing happening in your life of form justifies this. You will have insights and answers that you didn't know that you needed. Some of these will take your mind in directions that you didn't know existed. You will find yourself shifting to a deeper peace when it seems that you have done nothing to make this occur. When you sincerely invite Truth into your awareness It brings to your mind what you need to experience peace. This is why your only part in attaining peace is inviting Truth into your awareness.

At the very minimum the practice of simply quieting your mind everyday will be relaxing. Eventually, however, you will find that communing with Truth at least once a day will lead to you going about your day in peaceful contemplation. You will rest in the quiet center of your mind as you let the world and all of the personal thought system's thoughts about it go on around you.

2. Habit #2 Turn Within to Truth Throughout the Day

"I turn within to remember that only the Truth is True."

Your experiences of the world will close over your experiences of peace if you do not take time out several times a day to remember the Presence of Truth in your mind. Become present to Truth as soon as you can after you awaken in the morning and just before you go to bed at night. In between you can do this anytime anywhere because your mind is always free. You can turn inward while in the middle of a conversation with another, driving, working, shopping, in a meeting, playing with your kids, watching TV, water skiing, watching a sunset, etc. Take just a brief moment to come into the present and touch the Truth within. You don't have to close your eyes to do this. It is simply a moment of turning your mind inward. If you do have the time you can close your eyes for a minute or two to rest in Truth. The length of time that you take is not important. But your willingness to allow Truth into your awareness will determine whether or not you experience peace.

These moments should not be empty gestures because you think that you "should" do them. They are for maintaining your awareness of Truth so that you will flow through the day on a river of peace. This is your motivation for them. You might have to remind yourself of this if you find yourself resistant. Don't just say that you remember Truth, but call up your awareness of Truth by remembering other moments of being aware of Truth and peace. Remind yourself that peace is always right here, whether you feel it or not.

This practice is most important when you find yourself getting caught up in a painful drama appearing in the world, whether it seems to be "your" drama or "someone else's" drama. In fact, if you practice this enough appearances of discord will become reminders of Truth for you so that they will no longer disrupt your peace. You will maintain a state of peace because loving appearances remind you of Truth and discordant appearances remind you to remember Truth. This is how you can use the universe of form to maintain your peace of mind instead of to disrupt it.

It is important for your peace to return your mind to the awareness that only the Truth is True when you have been much occupied with something in the world. Preoccupation with the world leads to further preoccupation with the world. You want to break the spell and return to centering yourself in Truth as soon as possible. Use the normal transitions in the day, like when you switch from one task to another, from one location to another, take a break from activity, or simply find yourself with a quiet moment. In time when you find yourself "with a moment" to yourself you will automatically become present and turn your mind inward.

Practicing this habit will eventually result in you feeling that peace is with you always, no matter what is appearing in the universe of form.

3. Habit #3: Call on the Teacher of Truth for Guidance

"Teacher of Truth, I am open to Your guidance."

Before you look out at the universe of form you always look inward and choose one of the two thought systems in your mind. When you look at form from the personal thought system, however, you do not acknowledge that you first look inward, make a choice, and then interpret form. When you choose the personal thought system you choose to deny your own power. It seems, then, that whether or not you experience peace is a result of what happens to the personal self from a world outside of it rather than from your own choice. But when you look at form from your True thought system you consciously acknowledge that your experience is determined by your choice. First you choose peace then you look outward and interpret form. So for you to be at peace you must learn to identify with your True thought system. Otherwise you will think that lasting peace is beyond your reach and can only happen to you if some arbitrary power outside of you determines that you should have it.

As the Teacher of Truth in your mind your True thought system is a bridge between formless being (Truth) and your mistaken perception that you are form in a universe of form (not-Truth). The universe of form is a projection of not-Truth that not-Truth uses as a screen onto which to project itself. But form is neutral and has no meaning in itself. So, if you choose, the Teacher of Truth can use your perception of form to remind you of the Truth in your mind. This changes the world for you from a means for conflict through denial of Truth into a means to remember Truth and be at peace. With Truth as your guide the world becomes a bridge that leads you out of your belief in the reality of not-Truth and back to Truth.

If you want peace you must turn the Teacher of Truth in your mind into your Constant Companion in your perception that you are a person in a world. You must bring to Truth not only your spiritually-oriented questions but your practical questions and your goals and desires. This is not because what the personal self does in the world is real or affects Truth. It is because while you still believe in the world you must use it to experience Truth and learn to trust It. Using that in which you already believe, though erroneous, is Truth's means of gently and lovingly awakening you from your error to Truth and peace.

The Teacher of Truth uses this process because It is Love. It works lovingly with what has value for you until you let it go naturally as you learn that Truth and peace are more valuable. If It insisted that you give up a personal identity, your belief in a universe of form, and your attachment to these, you would have a sense of sacrifice. This type of thinking is exactly what the Teacher of Truth undoes. Not only would insisting that you give up what you want before you are ready to do so reinforce guilt and sacrifice in your mind, but it would result in you resisting Truth rather than opening to It. Remember, your belief in and attachment to not-Truth is a mistake that has an effect on your state of mind but not on Truth. It is not a "sin". You have done nothing wrong so the Teacher of Truth cannot teach you that you have. The Teacher of Truth is in your awareness because you have chosen to be at peace and for no other reason.

When you give over to the Teacher of Truth the personal self's life in the world every situation becomes one in which you can learn of peace rather than of fear. Eventually, as Truth becomes real to you and you value peace more and more, your belief in and attachment to the universe of form will fall away from you automatically. Any time that you have a sense of guilt or sacrifice you can be sure that you are listening to the personal thought system.

Beyond transforming the purpose of form from conflict to peace, calling on the Teacher of Truth has another advantage for you. It relieves you of the guilt and fear that come from identifying with not-Truth. When you experience the Truth within you it undoes the idea that you have "killed" Truth. So you undo the source of guilt and fear in your mind.

Over time you will call on the Teacher of Truth and learn to trust It. It will become your Constant Companion. As your awareness that Truth is always within you grows your identification will shift from the personal thought system toward your True thought system. Your sense of a *Teacher* of Truth will fall away as Truth will seem less "other" and more real within you. Your awareness of Truth will become unshakable and the source of your inner peace as the universe of conflict, chaos, and loss fades into the background of your mind.

4. Habit #4: Allow Love to Extend Through Your Mind to Remember That You Are Love

"I extend Love to remember that I am Love."

The thought system with which you identify automatically extends in your awareness. When you identify with a personal thought system this takes the form of the belief that you are a limited personal self in a limited universe of form. You feel the lack and vulnerability that this entails. The personal self's behavior is then needy and defensive. The world is a real place to you where you must fight for what you need or want. And you are constantly protecting what little you have.

When you identify with your True thought system, however, you are present to the Truth within you. You feel whole, happy, and at peace. Extending love, then, happens automatically. You are secure and giving, but not because it is "right" or "good" to be giving. Nor are you giving to get or to defend anything. Giving is simply the natural expression of knowing that you have everything without limit. You perceive the universe of from as a classroom where you learn over and over to let go of not-Truth in all of its forms and to remember that Truth and peace are reality. When you have perfected this lesson form falls away from your mind.

When you are not in touch with the Truth within you, you can consciously choose to get in touch with It by extending love in your awareness. The personal thought system responds instantaneously to any appearance, often with fear and loathing. You will hear the personal thought system as long as you are attached to any part of it. But if you want peace you do not want to let it have the last say. You can use situations in which the personal thought system responds un-lovingly to remember the Love within you. You do this by consciously choosing to extend love instead of the personal thought system's projections. You do not want to repress the personal thought system's judgments, which will only bury them in your subconscious. Nor do you need to punish yourself for them because they are not "wrong". They are only obstacles to peace for you. So let the personal self have its say, let it go, and choose to come from Love instead.

At first you might feel that you are practicing a form of denial. You might wonder how you can extend love to an appearance of ugliness, violence, or seeming threat. But remember that anything that happens in the universe of form is neutral. You respond only to the personal thought system's projections of meaning onto form. In other words, from the personal thought system you respond only to its thoughts. You never respond to what is actually appearing, which has no meaning in itself. So you can change the purpose of anything that you see in form from a validation of not-Truth to a reminder of Truth.

For example, you are walking in a section of a city where there are many homeless people on the street. The personal thought system's response to this appearance may be many things: disgust, pity, compassion, fear, anger, guilt, etc. Its response comes from whatever story you have accepted for homelessness, for the world in general, and/or for the personal self with which you identify. This gives meaning to the appearance and makes it real to you. Your thoughts may be about a specific aspect of the appearance, for example, "He's young and fit enough. I bet he's just too lazy to get a job." or "I can tell she's mentally ill. She might attack me!" Or your mind may run to more general thoughts about the appearance: "I could be homeless. Why them and not me?" or "This is why I hate capitalism."

After the personal thought system has its say you choose to use the appearance of homeless people as an opportunity to remember Truth. You do this by extending Truth in your awareness: "Only Love is real. I will see Love in place of this appearance." You might imagine light or some other symbol of Love in or around the people living on the street. Or you might simply turn your mind inward to Truth and remember that It is True. In any case, when the Truth comes into your awareness you feel uplifted, happy, and whole. Perhaps Truth moves through you and you smile or spontaneously touch or give money to one of the homeless people. Or you are not inspired to take any action at all. You turn away feeling completely secure in the awareness that the Truth in your mind beyond the images that the body's eyes report to you is all that is True. The personal thought system's fearful thoughts about the homeless people are replaced by gratitude for an opportunity to remember Love.

The personal thought system's constant lament is "What's in it for me?" So it may take you some time to sort out when your actions are coming from guilt and fear and when they are coming from a true awareness of the abundance of Love within you. The personal thought system will want you to give to others to feel good about yourself or to receive praise from others or from an authoritarian god. But this is not giving from Love. It is giving from guilt and fear. There is nothing wrong with this because it has no effect on Truth. But it will increase guilt and fear, not an awareness of Love, in your mind.

Always remember that behavior follows from thought, so behavior is never the source of your peace. If you behave in a certain way to get something, tangible or intangible, you are acting from the personal thought system. Behavior that results from your True thought system, however, is simply an automatic effect in form that has no purpose in itself.

You may feel that you are denying reality when you choose to extend Love in place of the personal thought system's projections. To move past this you must learn to watch how your mind chooses peace or conflict before it interprets form. You will only find peace through this honest examination and by making the choice for Truth over not-Truth. There is no other way because peace is the result of your awareness that only the Truth is True.

III.

The Process of Attaining Inner Peace

Introduction

Once you sincerely invite Truth into your awareness It takes you to peace. You will embark on a process of undoing your belief in, desire for, and attachment to not-Truth. The only part that you will play is in how easy or how difficult you make this process for yourself. The more that you invite Truth into your awareness, trust It to lead you, and accept the process, the easier it will be for you.

One instance of truly knowing that the Truth is True will be enough to set you on your way. This experience may come to you through your conscious or unconscious invitation. You may have a very strong or a subtle awareness of it. You may have had this experience before picking up this book. If this is the case the process has already begun for you. This book will have come into your awareness to help you understand what you accepted. Or this book may be what inspires you to open yourself to Truth and begin the process to inner peace. In essence, once you experience Truth you can say that the reality of peace has come into your awareness and that you are learning how to accept only peace in your mind and experience.

At first peace will seem to be a rare experience for you. Then it will become an occasional experience. Eventually you will have comprehensive peace, and, finally, total peace. The only thing that you have to do in this process is keep yourself centered in Truth. This is what the four habits in the previous section are for. Your obstacles to peace will arise naturally, and with the Teacher of Truth in your mind you will undo them. Each stage that you go through will follow naturally from the one before. You cannot force yourself into any stage. All that you have to do is trust and let the process unfold.

Be patient with yourself and the process. If you are committed to inner peace it may take two decades or more before you experience comprehensive peace. If this seems long to you do not despair. Your experiencing peace is not really contingent on time but on your willingness. Only in time does attaining peace seem to take time. Right now in this moment you can turn inward away from time, open yourself to Truth, and experience peace. The more that you do this the more that you will be at peace. The process of attaining inner peace, then, is one of releasing from your mind the part of it that thinks that it is in time so that the peace of Timelessness is all that remains.

Remember you are releasing from your mind a thought system with which you have been almost wholly identified. Everything that seems to surround you seems to support the reality of this thought system. You are re-training your mind to look inward for peace, not outward where you are used to looking for it. For a long while, before you recognize that you live only in your own thoughts, you will feel that you are swimming against the tide of a very real world. Moreover, in its attempts to hold your attention the personal thought system will go to any lengths to tempt you or to scare you away from Truth. It will even tell you that you are choosing your own death by choosing peace. But you will only be tempted and frightened by the personal thought system to the extent to which you still think that it is you. Its seeming hold over you, then, will be strong in the beginning and lessen over time. Eventually you will hear it but no longer listen to it. When you have released it completely it and its world will no longer exist in your mind at all. Your mind will know only peace.

Because your seemingly-individual mind seems to be unique the particular forms that your belief in, attachment to, and desire for not-Truth take will seem to be unique. So the process of undoing not-Truth in your mind that you undertake with the Teacher of Truth will be individualized for what seems like your particular mind. However, in general you can expect to go through the stages that follow. Keep in mind that these stages overlap and blend into each other: There will be no clear moment where you are in one stage and then in the next stage.

1. Conflicted

This initial period is long and very uncomfortable. But it is not without its moments of peace. You can reassure yourself with the awareness that once you pass this stage the process will never be this uncomfortable again.

This stage is often preceded by a sort of brief honeymoon as you first accept Truth into your awareness. This can go on for a few weeks or months. It may go on for longer. You will experience the peace and joy of accepting Truth into your awareness, so it may seem to you as though you have reached your goal. But really you will have only just accepted it. You will have yet to undo everything in your mind that stands in the way of you being wholly at peace.

a. The Conflict

You may think when the honeymoon is over that the conflict of which you become aware is new, but it is not. It is just that now you are looking directly into your conflicted mind. The personal thought system obscures, denies, or projects the conflict in your mind, so you are not used to looking right at it. Also, you have experienced peace, so you have an experience with which to contrast the conflict in your mind. You now know that peace is available to you, so conflict is no longer something to which you have to adjust. You know that you have a choice. Since nothing outside of you changed to bring you peace you are now aware, even if only dimly, that peace does not come to you from something outside of you. This is the exact opposite of the way in which you are used to thinking in your identification with a personal self.

Moreover, the personal thought system in your mind is aware that, even if only briefly, your attention has gone elsewhere. It cannot know or go to this other part of your mind. But it does know that your attention, which is its source of power, is capable of being withdrawn. It is threatened, so once you turn your mind back toward it, even slightly, it will go on the attack to keep your attention. This will increase your sense of conflict. Attack can take a form that looks like attack, for example, pushing whatever fear and insecurity buttons that you have or keeping your preoccupied with those things in your life that make you unhappy. Or it can take a form that is not so obviously an attack, like a burst of creativity, a new "love", distracting fantasies and plans, etc. In the beginning the personal thought system will use obvious forms of attack that tear you down. This will only motivate you away from it, however, so it will soon use subtler, disguised forms of attack that are designed to make you "feel good" in your identification with a personal self.

These attacks will be successful against you for a long time because you will be used to thinking that the personal thought system is really you. You will feel that its story for you is the truth. You will experience a sort of backlash to the personal thought system every time that you have a moment of Truth, like a period of brief peace or an insight that shifts you toward an awareness of Truth. These backlashes will seem to come to you unbidden, but really you will be choosing them on an unconscious level. You will make this choice because you will not wholly trust Truth yet. You will also fear that Truth will punish you for accepting a peace that the personal thought system tells you that you do not deserve.

Remember that the personal thought system's power source is your belief that it is real. Its seeming existence is the "evidence" that Truth has been overcome. In your identification with it you believe that you are a "sinner" against Truth. You feel unworthy of Truth and of the wholeness, love, peace, and joy that are the experience of Truth. You fear that Truth is out to get you. As a personal self you will never feel that you have paid enough for your "sins". You will be particularly frightened of Truth when you feel that you have experienced undeserved "good", either from the world or from Truth.

You will not be able to look directly at this guilt and the fear that it causes you until Truth and peace are very real to you. This occurs in the stage *Choosing Truth over not-Truth*. But you will see evidence that guilt and fear are in your mind in your own perceptions that guilt and fear are real in you or in others. Any guilt and fear that you perceive as real originates in your belief that not-Truth is real.

Truth will seem like something "other" to you in your identification with a personal self. So another aspect of your conflict at this stage is your sense that turning to Truth means giving up your power to another will. You will feel that calling on the Teacher of Truth in your mind is submitting to something outside of you rather than that you are claiming your True Power. At this stage it seems like you are stuck in a catch-22. Only an awareness of Truth will help you undo the guilt and fear that make you too afraid to turn to Truth to undo them. Your lack of trust in Truth is the very core of your discomfort. This is why this stage takes so long. It is a stage of faltering, stuttering steps, but it is obviously necessary. Trust in Truth does not grow overnight but only as you see justification for it.

Because of your continuing conflict you will continue to seek for relief through the personal self in the thoughts, attitudes, pleasures, pursuits, and behaviors that you have been used to using. You may also engage in diverse spiritual study. This will be largely an intellectual exercise for you at this point. You will probably be inconsistent with any spiritual practice, like the four habits. Both study and practice will seem to have little results as far as your experience of peace is concerned. But actually everything that you do to understand and open yourself to Truth will be helpful. Spiritual teachings cannot convey Truth to you, but they can motivate you to open to Truth by reassuring you that Truth is here and that It is Benevolent. You may not believe in this strongly, but you will believe in it enough to open yourself, however infrequently, to the Truth and peace. All of these moments of peace, both singly and collectively, will eventually result in your greater awareness of and trust in Truth. This is how you will experience peace more and more.

Later in this stage when you have reached a point of intellectually understanding spiritual principles the personal thought system will try to convince you that you are further along than you are. It has no problem with you studying spiritual teachings because it can distort them to increase your guilt. It is your experience of Truth, which it cannot touch, that threatens it. It will want you to stop looking further into your mind. And if you believe that you are more advanced than you are you will stop looking inward for your obstacles to peace. You will be motivated to listen to this because you will still believe, largely unconsciously, in your guilt. It will seem too vast or horrible to confront.

Your glimpses of peace coupled with your fear of looking within will make you sometimes desperate to be further along in your awareness of Truth than you are. But you cannot force yourself to an awareness that you simply do not have. It comes only as you work through your obstacles to it. The personal thought system may say that your intellectual understanding of spiritual concepts is all that you need. But only an awareness of Truth as Truth will cause in your mind an actual shift toward peace. It takes time to build your awareness of Truth and to trust It.

There will be times when your conflict is so great that you will regret inviting Truth into your awareness. You will ask yourself why you should bother with this process if nothing that you do or don't do as a personal self affects the Truth in your mind in any way. This is when you want to remember that peace is the natural state of being. When you are not at peace you inevitably seek for it. So the only real question is: Are you going to turn inward and find peace or continue to seek for peace outside of yourself where you will never find it?

The only way to peace is through an awareness of Truth in your mind. This requires that you undo the obstacles to your awareness of Truth. This can be an uncomfortable process, but it does get easier as you go along.

<u>b. External Shifts</u>

What shows up in your awareness of a universe of form is a mix of your conscious and unconscious desires. So your new goal of peace will result in shifts in the personal self's life in the world. These shifts will occur naturally as your values change. You do not have to force them. How much will change to reflect your new goal depends on how authentic is the life that the personal self is already living. How painful these shifts are depends on how attached you are to the people, things, situations, and roles in the personal self's life.

It is not uncommon for one to experience divorce, bankruptcy, foreclosure on their home, business failure, job or career changes, etc. when they truly accept peace as their goal. This may occur for one or two reasons. One has come to realize that those things to which they used to look for peace (a person, money, ambition, recognition, material things, etc.) cannot provide it. Those things naturally fall away as they no longer serve the purpose for which they were originally attained. Or one has not been directing the personal self to live an authentic life, which can be an obstacle to peace.

An *inauthentic life* is where a personal self lives a life that is not true to its nature. This is the result of personal guilt and fear in one's mind, which shows up as one feeling that the personal self is unworthy, wrong, bad, or sinful. They project this self-judgment onto others and/or their god so that it seems that the judgment is coming from outside of their own mind. They deny and repress the personal self's true human nature to appease their guilt. For example, a homosexual woman pretends to be heterosexual because she thinks homosexuality is a sin against her god. A man who does not want to raise a family gets married and has children because his culture tells him that this is what he must do. An artist from a family of lawyers goes into law to please his family when he would rather study and practice his art. A woman stays in a job that she loathes because it pays a large salary that inflates her self-esteem. Personal feelings of unworthiness, guilt, and fear that result in an inauthentic life are often the first obstacles to peace through which one must work when they let Truth into their awareness.

An authentic life is not Truth in itself. But the less guilt that you have about the personal self the more likely you are to feel worthy of Truth. This makes you less afraid of Truth and therefore more willing to open to It. This does not mean that you do not still experience the guilt and fear that are at the core of the personal experience. But it does mean that you have fewer layers of feelings of unworthiness and sinfulness to work through first.

It is ironic, but some level of personal self-esteem is necessary for you to open to Truth and undo your identification with a personal self. This is why some processes in the world that validate not-Truth-as-reality, like traditional psychotherapy and 12-step or other self-help programs, can be a necessary start to accepting Truth and experiencing peace. These processes have limits if you see them as ends in themselves. But they are useful as part of a larger process of preparing to accept Truth.

It is important to note that nothing in the world is responsible for your feelings of guilt and fear. These are symptoms of your belief that not-Truth is True. They are inherent in the personal identity into which you seem to have been "born". In other words, while parents, religious institutions, or your culture may reinforce ideas like guilt, unworthiness, or sinfulness, they are not the source of those ideas. Those ideas are in every personal thought system. You only accept reinforcement of them from "out there" because they reflect what you already believe from the personal thought system within you. You still have those feelings even if you seemed to have been raised in a loving, supportive environment. Only you have fewer layers of them through which to work. This is why those programs designed for making you feel good about yourself as a personal self never lead to complete peace. They can take you only so far in overcoming feelings of unworthiness and guilt. The next step would be you realizing that the personal thought system with which you identify is the source of these feelings, that it will not change, and that your only way out of conflict is to let go of the personal thought system completely. Those programs are not designed for the undoing of your identification with a personal self. Their goal is actually to reinforce not-Truth-as-reality in your mind while mitigating the pain of this mistaken belief.

An authentic life is one that is simpler. It requires much less effort for you to allow the personal self to live honestly than to direct it to live a life of denial and repression. These involve mind-consuming lies, distortions, subterfuges, and manipulations. An authentic personal self frees your mind to center itself in Truth.

When the personal self is authentic you are more open to Truth. And being aware of Truth will automatically lead you to allow the personal self an authentic life. This is because authenticity is the natural result of the undoing of the guilt and fear in your mind. So an awareness of Truth shows up in the world as a healthy, authentic personal self. This, in turn, makes it easier for you to remain aware of Truth.

The external changes that are the effect of you shifting your goal to peace may add to the discomfort that you are already experiencing from internal changes. But they occur to align the personal self in your mind with peace. Comfort yourself with the awareness that they will pass as the personal self's life resettles in a way that reflects peace. You will have other periods of shifting internally and externally as your commitment to peace deepens. But as time goes on you will accept them as part of the process. This, too, comes with trusting Truth to guide you to peace.

c. Re-evaluating the Idea of Sacrifice

Sacrifice is not-Truth's highest value. From its point of view you sacrificed Truth for it. Look at not-Truth's world and you will see how highly it values sacrifice, even unto one "dying for others". Sacrifice is the core value of its religions.

The personal thought system will tell you in many ways that Truth will require you to sacrifice for It. This is obviously a projection of its own values. You will accept this idea because of your own feelings of guilt. You will expect sacrifice to be demanded of you. This serves the personal thought system by making you fear and stay away from Truth. Sometimes you will hear outright thoughts that tell you that you must sacrifice. Often you will experience undefined fear in relation to Truth, and you will only find the thoughts of sacrifice behind the fear when you look for them.

The idea of sacrifice will show up with general thoughts, like giving up the personal self is a sacrifice. It will also show up with more specific thoughts, like being spiritual means the personal self living in poverty, giving up its relationships and desires, making choices that go against its nature, etc.

The idea that you must make some sacrifice to be "granted" peace is most intensely in your mind in this first stage. It adds to your sense of conflict. But throughout the process of attaining inner peace you will peel away many layers of the idea that sacrifice is necessary. The personal thought system is not going to release this idea, but you can release your belief in it. Look at the personal thought system's thoughts logically. Identifying with a personal self results in conflict and loss of peace. Is it a sacrifice to give up conflict for peace?

Also logically, would your awareness of Truth be likely to manifest as poverty or as the personal self's needs being met? Remember, the personal self is never supplied in the world by some external will. What shows up in the universe of form is an effect of your mind. As you grow aware of Truth you gain in peace. Peace does not show up as poverty and lack. Peace shows up as comfort and supply.

It is not the nature of Truth to oppose because It has nothing to defend. Does it make sense that the Teacher of Truth would work with what you believe or against it? It does not matter that your identification with a personal self is erroneous. What the Teacher of Truth knows is that you have asked for peace. It will meet you where you are right now to lead you to peace. The Teacher of Truth flows with not against what you think are your personal nature and desires. It uses them by turning them into the means for peace. Every situation in the world in which you find yourself becomes a classroom in which you learn to choose peace over conflict. Your attachment to personal desires will fall away naturally from your mind when you recognize that peace is more valuable than conflict.

Behind every form of resistance that you experience in relation to the four habits is the idea that you must make some sacrifice for peace. Do not let this idea go unexamined. Bring it to the surface in all of its forms. Look at it with the Teacher of Truth so that you can dispel it. The more that you experience Truth and peace the more that you will be reassured that Truth is Love. You will learn that peace does not demand sacrifice of any kind. The personal thought system will never teach you this. But you can learn it of Truth.

d. Developing an Awareness of the Teacher of Truth

This first stage to peace is all about becoming aware of the Teacher of Truth in your mind and learning to trust It. You will be almost wholly identified with a personal self, and the world will still be very real to you. You will be terrified of giving these up. As was just discussed, the personal thought system will tell you that you will be asked to sacrifice. This will make it very hard for you to trust the Teacher of Truth.

You are not asked to trust the Teacher of Truth without justification. The personal thought system is likely to increase your guilt by telling you that you are "bad" or "wrong" or "failing" to not trust the Teacher of Truth immediately. But the Teacher of Truth understands that you are hardly aware of It. It knows that your trust will develop only as you see justification to trust. Remember, Truth is. It does not require your awareness of It to be. So the Teacher of Truth's only investment in your awareness of It is your own desire for peace. Do not let the personal thought system tell you that you "should" just trust Truth or that you "should" trust It more than you have reason for yet. It is invested in you not learning to trust the Teacher of Truth. It will do anything that it can to distract you and tell you that you are failing.

At first you are likely to invite the Teacher of Truth into your awareness only when you are in pain or in crisis. From these experiences you will find that you can trust the Teacher of Truth to guide you away from pain and into peace. In time you will no longer wait for a crisis before you call on Truth. But you will still find it hard to believe that It won't ask you to sacrifice. In fact, you are really the one who is in charge of your awareness of the Teacher of Truth. You decide how much you want It in your awareness. You decide how much you are willing to give over to It to use to teach you peace. But this will take you a while to fully accept.

For a long time you will limit those situations where you call on the Teacher of Truth. You will hold back certain areas of your life where you are most attached to others, situations, or the roles that you play. But as you see the benefits of giving the Teacher of Truth the areas of your life where you are less attached you will realize that you want It in your awareness in all aspects of your life. Eventually you will know that you can turn to It with any question and you will receive an answer; with any pain and you will find relief. You will have gained enough trust in the Teacher of Truth to shift into the next stage.

2. Willing

It begins to get easier at this stage because you shift into a greater willingness to allow the Teacher of Truth in your mind to lead the way. This is not something that you can force or make happen. It is the natural result of you trusting the Teacher of Truth.

Your commitment to peace deepens. You are more certain that an awareness of Truth is what you want. You know that you always have the Answer with you, even if you still sometimes call on It later rather than sooner. All of this lessens your sense of conflict. Peace is still intermittent, but you begin to trust the process. You know that when peace is not in your awareness it will return again.

As you choose to follow only the Teacher of Truth in your mind your values will again shift. This will not be comfortable. But each time an old value falls away you will experience such relief that it will become easier for you to let them all go. The personal self will also experience some external shifts, but you will understand why they must occur. You will not be so resistant to them, so they will be less painful and they will go much smoother. This is all the result of your greater trust in the Teacher of Truth, Which becomes more and more your Constant Companion at this stage.

You may have thought before that you had made spiritual awareness your priority, but now it is truly so. You recognize that to be at peace practicing the four habits must take precedence over merely intellectually understanding a spiritual teaching. You are still very involved with the personal self, but you think of every situation in its life as a useful classroom where you learn of peace. So you are still more engaged in doing than in being, but the doing is with the Teacher of Truth leading the way. All of this doing is a useful part of your growing awareness of Truth.

At this stage your awareness of Truth means that that the personal self's relationships with others are more harmonious. Truth fulfills you and you know to turn to It when you are feeling incomplete or needy. So you no longer look outward to others to complete you or to make you happy. Rather than looking to the personal self's relationships as a source of love you recognize that loving relationships show up as the manifestation of your awareness of the Love within you. Some in your life will welcome this change in you, and if needed will change with you. Others will fall away as the changes in the dynamics of your relationship no longer suit them.

Your practice of the four habits becomes easier because you are willing to experience peace. Eventually, the four habits grow into your automatic response to everything that you encounter. In fact, your life becomes centered in them. You realize that whatever the personal self is doing in the world your awareness of Truth is your real purpose. You would no more be unaware of Truth than the body would not breathe.

At this stage you become more aware that the Truth is True, but you do not yet see clearly that not-Truth is not true. You seem to have two realities: the Truth within and the universe of form (not-Truth) that seems outside of you. You run to one when the other scares you, so you still remain in conflict. Truth still scares you because you have not yet undertaken the process of undoing the personal thought system's guilt in your mind. But you let Truth into your awareness more as you trust It more.

3. Comprehensive Peace

There comes a time where one day you look up and realize that a 'measure of peace has come to stay. You are not yet experiencing complete peace, but the peace that you do experience no longer ebbs and flows. It is always with you. Another way to put this is that the Teacher of Truth has become a Constant Presence. Inner peace and an awareness of Truth are the same experience.

Experiencing an unshakeable measure of peace motivates you to further center yourself in an awareness of Truth. Maintaining your peace becomes your purpose. You now want the Truth because It is the Truth. You look forward to the time that you give to Truth throughout the day.

At this stage your thinking is easier and clearer, too. You no longer think in terms of "my" mind and "other" minds. You realize that there is only one mind and it is in you. If a thought that evokes an emotional charge in you seems to come from another you realize that it reflects a thought in which you still believe and that you need to release.

You detach from the universe of form because you are more aware of the Truth within you. You no longer cling to personal pleasure or resist personal pain because you recognize that they both pass. You allow both to come and both to go. You are aware that you don't really live in a universe of form but in your own thoughts.

There are temptations at this stage. The peace that you have with you gives you a confidence that makes you feel that you can do anything with the personal self to which you put your mind. The personal thought system will take full advantage of this feeling. It will fill your mind with countless possibilities of what you could do and have with the personal self. You will experience a great depth of creativity and a sense of inner resources to pursue anything that you choose. But directing the personal self to act for personal fulfillment rather than watching its life unfold as you rest in an awareness of Truth will cost you peace. Peace has come to you from your awareness that the Truth is True. Pursuing not-Truth means abandoning this awareness. If you do give into the temptations of the personal thought system you will not do so for long. The loss of peace will be too painful, and you will quickly re-center your mind in Truth.

The personal self's life is simpler at this stage. You will continue to simplify it because your inner life is more real and more important to you. You have inner peace, so there is nothing for you to seek. Only complete peace lies ahead of you. This is a matter of choosing Truth over not-Truth in your mind right now.

You will become aware that everything that you have learned and acquired up through this stage was only preparation. You are about to embark on the real work of undoing your primary obstacle to peace: your attachment to the personal thought system.

4. Choosing Truth Over Not-Truth

This stage falls between comprehensive peace and complete peace, so it is the stage where you completely undo your belief in not-Truth. There are long stretches of peace here. Even when you experience conflict from your attachment to the personal thought system you still experience an abiding peace flowing alongside it. Peace has become the constant in your life.

You will realize that the personal thought system had its own agenda for your goal of inner peace. And this was part of your motivation to seek out Truth. You may have sought Truth to "spiritualize" the personal self with a role or self-concept. You may have wanted to be a "spiritual person" or "right" or "good". But peace is not personal. It is the natural result of letting go of the personal. You will find that you are willing to let go of all personal motivations for being aware of Truth. Otherwise they would continue to be obstacles to peace for you.

At this stage you finally uncover the guilt and fear at the center of the personal thought system. This will be very uncomfortable for you at times. But your awareness of Truth as Truth and the peace that this brings will release you from fear enough to look at the guilt in your mind and undo it. This undoing is that for which all the earlier stages prepared you.

You now turn inward and leave the universe of form behind. You are no longer attached to stories for yourself as a personal self in a world. Even the story that you had that supported your growing awareness of Truth will fall away. You will realize that all stories were bridges to bring your mind to this point and nothing more. The more that you live present to Truth, the more that you become aware that only the Truth is True. Everything else falls away.

As you identify more with Truth and peace and less with a personal self there will be fewer and fewer people in the world to which you relate.

But you will not be lonely. On the contrary, the peace that you experience is a feeling of completion. You experience no lack. You have nothing to seek for or to reach for. You have arrived at your goal of peace. Now all that you have to do is to fully realize this by letting go of the thought system that can only teach that lack is real.

The contrast between the personal thought system and your True thought system is stark now. You hear the personal thought system, but you listen to it less and less. You know that you only hear it because it is still in your mind. You realize, too, that you sometimes listen to it because you still want it. But you also realize that this does not change Truth. This awareness is your release. Even your desire for not-Truth is not True. It does not affect your inner peace because you sometimes get caught up in the personal thought system's stories for itself and its world. You simply release them again. The universe of form and your desire for it are really past for you.

The Teacher of Truth becomes less "other" and more simply your own mind at this stage. In fact, mind is more real to you than form. You deal now always with your thoughts, and you have no goal for the personal self. You recognize that it and its world are just ideas in your mind. You watch their stories unfold without attachment and with an open mind. You know that as an effect of your peaceful mind the story of form is unfolding perfectly, whatever is appearing at the moment. In fact, the personal self in your mind lives in the flow of peace.

Now you have only one goal and it is for your mind: to let go of all of your obstacles to complete peace.

5. Complete Peace

A state of complete peace means one without conflict. So it is a state of mind without any belief in or attachment to not-Truth. You may still hear the personal thought system and perceive its world for a while. But they have no more reality for you. Then the universe of form will fade away from your awareness as your mind melts into formless, boundless Truth. And only Truth and peace will be left.

IV.

Contrasting Concepts for Overcoming Obstacles to Peace

Introduction

Both Truth and not-Truth are in your mind. In your conflict you have confused the attributes of each with the other. This has led to you making not-Truth real to yourself and to you fearing Truth. These confused concepts function as obstacles to peace when you accept them without examining them through an awareness of Truth.

Some ideas that you need to sort out were discussed in Part I of this book. But there are many spiritual and metaphysical concepts that the personal thought system uses for its own purposes. It does this to keep guilt and fear in your awareness and to validate itself as real in your mind. What follows, then, is a look at the contrast between certain concepts to help you sort out Truth and not-Truth. When you understand the distinction between them you will be able to choose Truth over not-Truth and be at peace.

1. One Truth instead of Dualism

Formless Being has no beginning and no ending. It is eternal, or timeless. It is everywhere and always. It is the same throughout, or one within Itself. It is all that is, so It is the Truth.

Not-Truth is the opposite of Truth in every way. It is only an idea that was undone by Truth's all-encompassing nature the moment that it arose. It only seems real to you in your belief that time is real. It is nowhere, never. It is the idea that limited diverse form is real.

Even in your belief that the idea of not-Truth is reality Truth is always in your mind. So your mind seems split between Truth and not-Truth. While you want not-Truth your mind has two ways of dealing with this split. It can deny that Truth (formlessness) exists at all and insist that not-Truth (form) is reality. Or it can project the split as the belief in *dualism.* Dualism is the idea that reality consists of two equally true, opposing aspects. In this case, the universe of form and formlessness, sometimes called *spirit.* The purpose of the concept of dualism is to give not-Truth reality by raising it to the level of Truth. In fact, in the belief in dualism Truth (spirit) is often believed to inhabit not-Truth (body) in an attempt to blend them.

This belief, however, has nothing at all to do with what occurs when you actually do experience Truth. When you have a direct experience of Truth you experience only Truth. Not-Truth does not exist in Truth as even an idea. So the experience of Truth completely undoes the idea of not-Truth. If you do earnestly bring not-Truth together with Truth they do not blend. Not-Truth disappears from your mind.

Dualism only has meaning from the perspective of not-Truth and it is only ever an idea. In fact you cannot understand Oneness through the personal thought system. When you do experience Truth directly it is in a moment when you have put the personal thought system aside entirely so that only Truth remains in your mind. This is an experience of complete peace.

It may seem contradictory to say that not-Truth is only an idea then to say that in Truth it does not exist even as an idea. This is where experience trumps the limitations of the personal intellect. Only through the experience of Truth can you understand the nothingness of not-Truth. You will never grasp this through intellectual reasoning.

The concept of dualism also shows up in not-Truth in the belief that the universe of form is made up of two equal, opposing forces: light and dark or good and evil. The light or good forces are called *God* and the dark or evil forces are called *Satan.* Satan is the force in the universe that is supposed to be responsible for tempting innocent humans into "sinning" against God.

The concept of Satan is a symbol of not-Truth's opposition to Truth. The evil connotations for Satan are a projection of the personal thought system's guilt. On a personal level the value in believing in Satan is that you can see it as ultimately responsible for your guilt. You are just a poor, weak human who is overcome by a superior force into behaving in ways opposed to God. But the cost to you in this belief is that for this to be true you must believe that you are powerless to choose whether or not you experience peace.

It is true that your seemingly-individual mind is only a projection of one mind that thinks that it is split between Truth and not-Truth. But this does not make you powerless to choose what you want in your mind. There really is no difference between the mind that projects and its seemingly-individual projections of mind. All mind is mind. You have free will because Truth is your mind's reality and not-Truth is only an idea in your mind. So the choice is yours to make.

But in fact the choice in your mind is a false one. There is no real choice between What exists and what does not exist. This can only be an illusion of choice. Only the Truth in your mind is True. There is no dualism, only oneness, which is the same throughout itself and has no opposing parts. To be aware of this is to be at peace.

2. Formlessness instead of Emptiness

Truth is formless, so form of any kind is not-Truth. *Form* refers not only to material form that can be seen by the body's eyes but also to that which cannot be seen by the body's eye, like ideas, unseen forces, and energies. Anything that has limits or can be measured is form. Truth, or formlessness, can be directly experienced. But It can never be adequately conveyed in words or measured because limited form cannot capture limitless formlessness.

In not-Truth, then, Truth is referred to as *spirit*, a *void*, or *nothingness* because the experience of Truth is without form. To the personal thought system this means emptiness. However, Truth is nothing only in terms of form. In terms of your experience It is everything. Truth is something that you experience only within you. It is a wholly subjective experience.

You will not understand Truth through the personal thought system. Ideas and concepts, which are limited form, may motivate you to open to Truth. This is the value in spiritual study when you want inner peace. But you will never understand Truth through the personal intellect. Only by opening your mind to Truth, Which is within your mind always, will you experience It and be at peace.

3. Universal Truth instead of Personal Specialness

When you experience Truth you experience the wholeness and limitlessness of the one Being that is. So when you turn inward to Truth in your seemingly-individual mind you turn to the exact same Truth in any other seemingly-individual mind. Truth is universal. It is the universality of Truth that makes It True. Truth cannot sometimes be something else and still be True.

As not-Truth the personal experience is the opposite of Truth. It is a unique, or "special", expression of lack and limitation. What is "true" for one personal self is "not true" for another. What is "true" for one personal self at a given time may be "not true" for that same one at another time. It is this lack of universality that makes not-Truth not True.

a. Guilt and Specialness

Every concept of a personal self is unique or "special". While all personal thought systems are the same in content—not-True—each seems to be original. All personal selves are fearful, insecure, defensive, and selfish. They also wear masks of confidence, friendliness, helpfulness, and innocence to hide or to serve these traits. How these traits blend in each, however, is exclusive to each. For example, one might be overtly insecure where another's insecurities are more subtle. One might live in a state of constant anxiety where another has only bouts of conscious anxiety. One is violently defensive where another defends their self through passive-aggressive behavior.

The outer form of the personality and body of a personal self is also a distinctive blend of traits. And each idea of a personal self seems to be "born" into a specific set of circumstances that might resemble another's but is never exactly the same as any other's.

In your identification with a personal self you may ask, "Why was I born into this dysfunctional family?" or "Why was I blessed with this musical talent?" But there is no answer. The personal self wants a personal explanation for its special traits and circumstances to validate itself as real. But it is never real. It is only a passing idea. There is no explanation for what is never real and has not really happened. Each personal self is a random expression of the-opposite-of-Oneness. It does not come from Truth. So its traits are not "God-given" or "meant to be". Any personal self that you think about has no inherent meaning or purpose. Any meaning that you ascribe to a personal self comes from your mind.

Since a personal identity is not-Truth it is the idea that Truth has been undone. This is why guilt is inherent in a personal thought system and in anything to do with a personal self. Any attachment that you have to specialness—yours or another's—means your attachment to the personal identity and guilt. Guilt also lurks behind any questions that you may have about any seeming-specialness.

When you are unhappy with the random circumstances into which the personal self was "born" the personal thought system will tell you, consciously or unconsciously, that it is because you are being punished. This is either for sinfulness in general or for something specific in a "past life". This interpretation serves the personal thought system in two ways. It perpetuates your sense that guilt is real. This makes you afraid to look within and find Truth. And it uses your feeling that your circumstances are consequences of either general sinfulness or of a past life as "proof" that the personal thought system exists beyond its short seeming-life.

When you feel blessed by the random circumstances or traits into which the personal self was "born" you feel guilty because many do not share in a similar blessing. You may hide your guilt behind blustery self-confidence or a declaration of inherent entitlement. You may resort to punishing the personal self to balance out your sense of undeserved fortune. Or you may take on more responsibility in the world in "payment" for your good fortune. But none of these behaviors will undo guilt. They only validate guilt as justified.

A personal self has special traits from the beginning and develops special traits in the course of its "life". The personal self in your awareness may be especially "good" or especially "bad". It may be especially "blessed" or especially "cursed". Perhaps it is the best victim or the best victimizer. However specialness shows up your attachment to it will only enhance your guilt. This is not because of the specific traits or circumstances, but because you believe that the personal self is real. It is this belief that is the source of all guilt in your mind. You cannot escape from within the personal thought system the guilt that you feel for being special. You can only escape all guilt by releasing yourself from identifying with a personal self. Then only the Truth will be in your mind and you will be at peace.

b. Eternal Life instead of Life After Death

Truth has no beginning and no ending. It is infinite. So questions about beginnings and endings always originate in not-Truth, are always about not-Truth, and are meant to reinforce the mistaken belief that not-Truth is True.

The personal thought system often asks questions that are not really questions but are statements in the form of questions. This is most evident with the question, "What happens when I die?" This question is based on the faulty premise that that which is asking the question exists. So there is no way to answer it directly without validating the faulty premise. This is why the question is really the personal thought system's way of stating that it exists.

When a question arises in your mind you must ask yourself, "What is asking?" All questions come either from the personal thought system or the seemingly-individual mind in which the personal thought system seems to be. The personal thought system's questions are never open to real answers. Its questions are only meant to validate itself. But your seemingly-individual mind is open to real answers from your True thought system when you are willing to put aside the personal thought system.

While your seemingly-individual mind is also not-True it is the means through which you learn while you still seem to have to learn. Truth is whole and complete, so in Truth you have nothing to learn. But while not-Truth is in your awareness you seem to have to learn that only the. Truth is True.

When you choose peace you return to an awareness of Truth through the individual mind. But eventually the individual mind will fall away from your awareness and only Truth will remain. So first you learn that the personal thought system is not you but is an idea in your mind. You also learn about Truth, Which is your mind's reality. It is represented in your seemingly-individual mind by your True thought system. As you sort out the two thought systems in your mind you practice making the choice between them. This lesson eventually generalizes. You recognize that you are not one split mind among many split minds but that there is only one seemingly-split mind which seems to have taken many forms. You no longer experience mind as "my mind", "your mind", and "their mind", though the personal self still necessarily communicates in these terms with seeming-others.

Individuality, then, falls away from your mind. You realize that there is no individual soul or spirit or mind that "continues on" or "reincarnates" after the "death" of the personal self. The individual and personal are only erroneous ideas that take many forms. So you must release your attachment to them to be at peace. When you do release them it is not "you" as a personal self or as an individual mind that does so. It is "you" the one mind that made the mistake of thinking that it is split. This mind transcends the personal and individual in the recognition that Truth is Universal. There is only one Mind. Being aware of this is not "death" but Life in Its truest sense.

So when a personal self seems to "die" nothing happens in Truth just as nothing happened when it seemed to be "born". It was the erroneous idea that not-Truth-is-true given the form of a body. Every seemingly-individual mind that perceived that body projected onto it a personality and story that was meaningful to itself. The body is no longer perceived to receive the projections, so other personal selves are left only with "memories" of the personality and story that they had projected. These, too, are just further projections from their own minds. Neither the body, the personality, the story, or the minds that projected all of these are real. Only the Truth is True, eternally. And it is in this realization that you find peace and release from all concerns with "death".

c. The Enlightened Mind

Enlightenment is the label given to an inner awareness of Truth. The True thought system in your mind is aware of Truth, so it is enlightened. The personal thought system, which is not-Truth, can never be aware of Truth. It can never become enlightened. When you are attached to it, it functions as an obstacle to your awareness that you already have enlightenment. So you do not have to seek for enlightenment. You only have to release the personal thought system and the Enlightened Mind will be all that is left in your awareness.

Truth is universal, not personal or individual. So there is no such thing as "personal enlightenment" or an "enlightened person". When your seemingly-individual mind is aware of Truth it transcends the personal and individual in the awareness that Truth is All. Then the boundary of "individual" drops away from your awareness. This applies not only to yourself but for seeming-others as well. When you are aware of Truth you disregard the personal or individual everywhere. You are aware of only the Universal.

If you think that you know of an "enlightened person" then you can only be thinking with the personal thought system. As distinct form the personal thought system cannot think in general or universal terms. It cannot conceive of one being as Truth. The only value that the concept of *enlightenment* has for it is to single out individuals as special. Certainly it is willing for you to be special as an "enlightened person". This is its only motivation in "allowing" you to seek Truth.

But if you are not ready to exalt yourself as an "enlightened person" it is happy to have you submit yourself to another "enlightened" personal self. It actually prefers that you seek Truth in another than that you seek Truth within yourself because you might accidently discover that the

Truth is within you. It always prefers that you seek for Truth outside of you where you will never find It.

No one outside of you can convey Truth to you. You may find teachers who model a greater awareness of Truth than you have for the time being. But if they are truly teachers of Truth they will point you inward, not to themselves.

The split mind always has Truth in it. So Truth breaks through into the story of not-Truth as historical figures who were aware of Truth. The stories for these people are no more real than the story that you have for the personal self in your awareness. But the Teacher of Truth in your mind can use their stories as allegories or as models for becoming aware of Truth. And if you find that the idea of a Teacher of Truth within you is too abstract you may find one of these historical teachers embodying the Teacher of Truth for you. But these stories and symbols are only temporary comforts as you work through guilt and fear of Truth. If you are actually following Truth in these forms they will lead you to the formless Truth within you and fall away.

Only a personal self is concerned with labels or roles or with being a certain kind of person. A person who considers themselves "enlightened" is spiritualizing the personal self with which they identify. They are trying to give not-Truth the attributes of Truth. If their mind was truly enlightened they would have no need to declare this. To whom would they declare it? They would no longer conceive of anything but Truth. There would be nothing with which to compare their awareness of Truth so no need to give it a label.

When applied to a person the term *enlightened* only has meaning as a judgment against which to evaluate the unenlightened. And what would make such a judgment but a personal thought system that can never be enlightened? So seeking to be an enlightened person or seeking for an enlightened person to follow both function as obstacles to peace. Turning inward to Truth and finding Universal Enlightenment Itself is the only way to lasting peace.

4. Mind as Cause instead of Mind as Effect

It is the Law of Mind that mind knows only itself. In Truth this means that Truth knows only Truth. Your True Mind is then both Cause and Its Own Effect. It is both Knower and What It knows. Truth is One.

Not-Truth cannot escape the Law of Mind. So to oppose the Law it denies the Law. In the part of Mind where the idea of not-Truth seems to be thought this split mind (cause) projects away its not-True thoughts as a universe of form (effect) so that they seem separate. The universe of form then no longer seems to be an idea in mind but seems to be a reality unto itself. But not-Truth cannot actually separate cause and effect, so it reverses them. The split mind projects itself into its effect as a multitude of individual minds. The split mind now seems to be many split minds in forms (bodies) in a universe of form which seems to have caused these minds.

So when you identify with a personal self in a body in a world you think that you are a form that was caused by a universe of form. You think that you are part of a continuum of form. You believe that your mind is an effect of a brain (form). You believe that your feelings of conflict or peace are the effect of what is happening in the world outside of you. Your mind seems to be an effect, not a cause.

Your split mind's seeming-reversal of cause and effect leaves you confused, conflicted, and feeling powerless. But it does not actually change what is cause and what is effect. Projecting the personal thought system's thoughts onto a universe of form does not rid your mind of its thoughts. You are obviously still aware of them. Projecting them away is only a means to deny that they are your thoughts.

So your first step out of the conflict that denial and projection cause is to take back your projections. You think that the world tells you what it means, but in fact the universe of form has no meaning in itself. All of the meaning that you see in it you project onto it. Invariably the meaning that you project from the personal thought system ties into the story that you have for yourself as a personal self. So step back and observe these projections. Notice how they tie into the story in your mind. Recognize how the universe of form only has meaning for you because of your thoughts about it. Then you will be able to release the thoughts, turn your mind inward to Truth, and be at peace.

When you are still identified with a personal self and you first learn that mind is cause and the universe of form is effect the personal thought system will try to use this awareness for its own ends. What follows is a look at some of the ways that it will do this so that you can sort out the personal thought system's distortions from the real way to peace.

a. The Law of Mind and Attracting, Creating, or Manifesting

It takes a long while to retrain your mind to recognize that your experience of conflict or peace is the result of your choice of thought system and not of what seems to be happening to the personal self. It requires consistent willingness to withdraw your mind from the world and to turn it inward. You must experience again and again the awareness that peace is a state of mind before this awareness will sink in.

So when you first learn that your mind is the cause of your experience the personal thought system will use this idea for its own ends. It will encourage you to use the Law of Mind to attract, create, or manifest what it tells you that the personal self needs in the world for you to be happy and peaceful. In other words, it will continue to reinforce in your mind the idea that what appears or not in the universe of form is the cause of your experience of conflict or peace.

What shows up in the universe of form for you is the result of your conscious and unconscious beliefs and desires. There is no mystery here. You are constantly making decisions in the world, both consciously and unconsciously. These decisions reflect your values. For example, when you changed your goal to inner peace you began to make decisions that reflect this new value. You directed the personal self to drop certain activities and relationships to make time for the study, meditation, and contemplation that are now more important to you. Making choices based on your values is automatic. In fact, if you want to know what you really value look at the choices that you make instead of what you say that you value.

This is how your values are manifested in the universe of form: You set a goal with your mind (cause) and this leads to choices that you make at the level of form (effect). Form, which includes behavior, follows thought. So first you decide (cause) that you want inner peace and then a more peaceful life for the personal self manifests (effect) as you make choices in line with peace.

Be aware of how the personal thought system will distort this awareness when something occurs in the universe of form that it judges as "bad" or "wrong". It will tell you that you are guilty since what shows up is an effect of your mind. But it will actually be its judgment of "bad" or "wrong" that causes your feelings of guilt. What happens in the universe of form has no meaning in itself.

For example, if you live in an area prone to earthquakes you are responsible for choosing to live there but not for manifesting specific earthquakes. Earthquakes are caused by the earth's crust shifting. This is simply the way that the earth functions. It has no meaning in itself. It is not "bad" or "wrong", and it is certainly not personal. So how you experience the earthquakes comes only from the meaning that you give to them. The meaning that you give (effect) depends on your goal for yourself (cause). This is either conflict or peace. If you want to be in conflict then you will use the earthquakes to reinforce guilt in your mind. You may see them as "bad" occurrences meant to punish you. Or you may listen to the personal thought system as it tells you that you are "wrong" for choosing to live where earthquakes occur. But if you choose peace you will accept the earthquakes as natural consequences of your living where earthquakes occur. You will not give meaning to them by using them for a story of personal guilt. You will know that peace comes from an awareness of Truth, not from what happens in the universe of form. You will trust that if you need to direct the personal self to make changes to keep it safe during earthquakes you will know to do so. If it's time to move the personal self to a less earthquake-prone place you will know to do that.

Your seemingly-individual mind does not live in isolation. It is a projection of one mind that it has never left. This one mind provides the macro story (universe of form) onto which the seemingly-individual mind projects its micro story (meaning). So your choices for the personal self ripple out into the macro story and the macro story responds to your choices. Most obviously your choices for the personal self affect those in whom it comes in contact, especially those closest to it. And they in turn respond to your choices. But also on an unseen level you attract to your micro story from the macro story of which it is a part opportunities, situations, and people to manifest your goal of either conflict or peace. This is automatic and ongoing. It is also meaningless for inner peace. What occurs in the universe of form is only an effect of your choice for conflict or peace. What does or does not show up is never the cause of your experience of conflict or peace. So no matter what is appearing if you are not at peace you can still make the choice for peace where it is, in your mind.

Only the personal thought system concerns itself with what does or does not show up in the universe of form. This is because it wants you to believe that the universe of form causes your peace or conflict. But it is a thought system of lack so the meaning that it projects onto form can only represent lack. When you identify with it you are never satisfied with what shows up and you whine about what is not showing up.

But your True thought system knows that what is or is not showing up is not your cause but is your effect. When you are centered in Truth you know that what shows up is the perfect expression of your inner peace. You take the longer view for the personal self, knowing that in the universe of form and limitation it cannot have everything at once. Wholeness is expressed in limited form through transformation. One form falls away to make way for another form that is a more appropriate expression of your current state of mind.

As you center your mind in Truth and peace becomes an ongoing experience within you, you will give less and less thought to the universe of form. You will let it unfold as it unfolds. You will not think about it because you cannot have two realities. Either the peace within or the universe of form is reality.

b. The Law of Mind and Physical Healing

Since the universe of form is an effect of the mind the body is an effect of the mind. Physical disorders and diseases, then, are caused by your mind and are removed by your mind. These thoughts are usually made unconsciously in an instant.

The body is a projection of the mind. It is the personal thought system given form. Its health or its disordered state is part of the personal self's story. Part of its story may be that its body was born with a disorder or deformity. Along the way its story will include injuries, disorders, and diseases, some lasting and some temporary.

The personal thought system has many uses for illness and injuries. It uses them to attract attention, to avoid someone or something, to get rest, to manifest your guilt, to punish you, to make others guilty, to play the martyr, etc. What shows up in the body or what happens to it through injury is the result of your conscious and unconscious beliefs and desires. As long as you are attached to the personal thought system in any way the conflict in your mind will manifest through the body as disorders, diseases, and injuries.

When you learn that physical disorders are caused by thoughts in your mind the personal thought system will lead you to feel guilt, anger toward yourself, and fear. It will tell you that this awareness exposes exactly how "bad" you really are. You will hate yourself for any disorders of the body. Of course, further guilt and blame only perpetuate the problem in your mind. They do not undo it, which is why the personal thought system uses them.

That what shows up in the body is the result of thoughts in your mind is simply a fact, not a justification for condemnation. A healthy body is no more your reality than a sick one is. Your identification with a body in any condition results in guilt because you believe that you have attacked Truth to make another reality. All that your awareness of a universe of form indicates is that you still have the personal thought system in your mind. This is not "bad". It is nothing. The personal thought system does not change the Truth in you. It is only an idea with no real effects. Its only power over you is what you give to it to have over you. And you give it power when you feel guilty about the body in any way. But you can empower yourself instead by choosing to use the appearance of disorders as reminders to turn your mind to Truth.

The personal thought system will also tell you that you should use the mind to heal the body. This does order cause (the mind) and effect (disorder in the body) correctly, but only in a limited sense. Using the mind to heal the body implies that you believe that identifying with a body is erroneous only when the body is in a disordered state. Otherwise you would not single out for healing only those thoughts that lead to disorder in the body. It also indicates that you believe that the body's state affects your state of mind. This again confuses cause and effect. Further, it reinforces in your mind the idea that mind exists to serve form, making both real to you.

Your conflict is never the result of a particular disorder that shows up but of your identification with a body. A disordered body is only a symptom of this. Healing a symptom does not undo the underlying cause of the symptom. Only by withdrawing your identification from a body and returning your mind to Truth will the body, as an effect of your mind, escape the disorders that are the consequences of you misidentifying with it. Mind does not exist to serve form. Form is an effect of mind.

When you attend to what is happening in the universe of form, including in the body, you choose conflict. But when you attend to your state of mind and work through your obstacles to being aware of Truth you choose peace. Either of these choices will manifest in the body's story in the world. But when you are at peace it will not matter to you what is or is not happening in the world of form, even in the body.

Since whether the body heals or not is an effect of your mind it is possible for the body to heal spontaneously. But it is more likely that healing will be represented in the body's story by external means, like physicians, treatments, and medicines (traditional or non-traditional). When you center your mind in Truth you will know how to direct the body when it needs something. You will become aware of the right diet, exercise plan, treatments for illnesses and injuries, etc. for the particular body in your awareness. This is the effect of your awareness of your wholeness in Truth. But until you choose only peace consistently on all levels of your mind discord and disease in the body will continue to manifest.

As you choose to be aware of the Truth because It is the Truth your mind will become more and more unified in peace. The healing and wholeness that shows up in the universe of form, including in the body, will be the effect of your harmonious state of mind. Then the universe of form will fall away completely from your mind.

c. The Law of Mind and True Power

Since only the Truth is True only in Truth can you be in touch with your own True power. As the opposite of Truth not-Truth is powerless in the most literal sense. Being only an idea it has no power at all. You can seem to give power to it, but then its seeming-power is only your projection of power onto it. An idea which seems to have power over you is actually empowered by you.

When you believe that you are a personal self in a body in a world you believe that your effect is your cause. You believe that you are powerless and that the universe of form has power over you. You are in a state of constant vulnerability, fear, and defensiveness. And in your powerlessness you believe that the only way that you can be empowered and at peace is to manipulate and control others and your environment. But this never works because you really react only to your projections of meaning. Even if your manipulations seem to work in one situation you will simply project fear into other situations. So to be truly empowered and at peace you must release your attachment to the story that you have for you as a personal self.

The insecurity that you experience when you identify with a personal self is not your own. It is the personal thought system's insecurity that you take on as your own. The personal thought system does not know that it does not exist. But it does know that it is not its own source. There is a power over it and it is you. This is why it is insecure. And this is why when you identify with a personal self the power that you fear is your own.

When your mind has been attending to Truth the personal thought system will do whatever it can to hold onto your attention when your attention returns to it. It will attack you with fearful thoughts. Or it will distract you with manifestations of appetites or pain in the body. Remember that it does not care if you love it or hate it as long as you believe in it. Just as you feel when you identify with it that you have to manipulate and control the world that you think is your source the personal thought system feels that it must manipulate and control you, who are its source.

Lack of power and acquiring power are not considerations in Truth. When you are aware of the Truth within you, you are in the State of Empowerment. Power, manipulation, and control are irrelevant concepts for you. You are at peace and you know that its Source is within you. So you have no need to manipulate or control anything. You are able to let go of the universe of form because you know that it is not your cause but your effect.

d. Extending Love instead of Fixing the World

It should be quite clear by now that the universe of form does not cause your experience of peace or conflict. This is determined by your choice of thought system. Each thought system in your mind approaches the world very differently. The personal thought system projects meaning onto it to make it real to you. Then it tells you that what you see in the world is fact and the cause of your conflict. Your True thought system overlooks the world because it knows that the world is a meaningless effect. It knows that the Cause of your peace is within you.

The personal thought system projects its own guilt and fear outward and concludes that you live in a frightening world where you are under constant attack. So it tells you that you need to fix the world to be at peace. Your True thought system rests within in its own love and extends its love outward because it is loving. It is motivated to extend love by its own abundance of love not because it believes in the lack that it perceives in the world.

So fixing, correcting, or trying to make the world a better place so that you can be at peace are means for maintaining in your mind the confusion of cause and effect. They are behaviors motivated by the idea that your experience of conflict or peace is caused by something outside of you. They do not undo your belief that not-Truth is real, which is the only way to lasting peace. When you understand that peace is a state of mind and that the universe of form is only an effect of your mind then what does or does not show up in the universe of form is irrelevant to you.

When you get caught up in what is appearing in the world turn inward to Truth and remember that only the Truth is True. As your awareness of this grows the universe of form will fall away from your experience as something real to which your mind must attend. The personal self's actions in the world will then be extensions of the peace and love in your awareness rather than an attempt to fix the world so that you can find peace and love in it.

Think of your mind with not-Truth in it as being like a finger with a splinter in it. The splinter is the foreign object in the finger, the presence of which causes it pain. To remove the pain from your finger you would not try to fix the splinter. You would remove the splinter so that your finger could be in its natural pain-free state. So it is with not-Truth in your mind. For your mind to be in its natural state of peace you must remove the foreign, pain-causing belief that not-Truth is your reality.

5. Sin as a Mistaken Belief instead of Sin as Reality

Sin is the idea that not-Truth has attacked Truth to make itself real instead. Of course this can only be a mistaken idea and not reality. But the personal thought system, which is not-Truth in your mind, can never accept that this is only a mistaken idea. This would mean its acknowledging that it does not exist. The idea that it is sin is at the very center of the personal identity. The guilt and fear of punishment that this belief inspires in you when you identify with it is essential to the personal thought system as a defense against the Truth. As long as you believe that you are sinful you will be too afraid to look within and see the guilt that you believe is there. And if you do not look within you will not find Truth. You will not be able to undo the personal thought system.

You do not need a religious background to believe in sin. This belief is at the center of every personal thought system. Some of not-Truth's religions only provide a context for the inherent guilt and fear that you experience in a personal thought system. Any time that you believe that guilt is real anywhere you believe that not-Truth is real, that it has undone Truth, and that the guilt in your mind is justified.

As long as you are attached to a personal identity you are attached to the belief that sin and guilt and impending punishment are reality. You are conflicted and afraid. You manifest various forms of punishment for yourself in the hopes that this will mitigate any punishment that Truth could bring down on you. But at any time you can choose instead to open yourself to Truth and learn that sin is only a mistaken idea with no reality. This is the choice for peace.

To the personal thought system the greatest sin that you can commit is to accept your eternal innocence. It will tell you that believing that you are innocent is arrogant and irresponsible. It is the ultimate infraction against not-Truth, its god. Believing this will be a source of great fear for you as you approach Truth. But you must be aware that it is in your mind to undo it. Remember that there is no personal thought system without guilt, and there is no guilt in your mind without the personal thought system.

a. Eternal Innocence and the World's Laws

Since the personal thought system can never really understand that sin is not real it can only play with this idea intellectually. It will facetiously say things like, "So I can lie and cheat and rape and steal and murder because these are not sin". Of course you only direct the personal self in these behaviors when you believe that sin is real. These behaviors are for getting something that you think you lack, and lack is only real to you when you believe that you are a personal self. And when you believe that you are a personal self you believe that sin is real. But when you are truly aware of your eternal innocence you know that there is no such thing as sin because you know that wholeness, not lack and limitation, is real. You have no motivation, then, to direct the personal self to engage in these behaviors.

The personal thought system may argue that since you are innocent in Truth then you do not have to direct the personal self to obey the world's laws. Of course its concern with the behavior of the personal self reveals that it does not really believe that you are innocent. It is saying that the personal self is you rather than an idea in your mind. So it is saying that you are guilty of attacking Truth. It is also indicating that your state of mind is determined by the world's laws. Otherwise it would have no idea with which to motivate you defy them or to try to change them.

When you are truly aware of your eternal innocence you know that the universe of form is not your source. So its laws are irrelevant to your state of mind. The personal self in your mind manifests as a healthy, mature individual living harmoniously within the world's laws.

The personal thought system may suggest that you not put the personal self in a position to sit in judgment on others—for example, on a jury—because you may be called upon to find another "guilty" when guilt is not real. This is "spiritualizing" not-Truth. This means applying the attributes of Truth to it. Eternal innocence applies only to Truth. Not-Truth is neither innocent nor guilty because it is nothing. The universe of form is only an idea, not a reality. Laws in the world are there for the civilized functioning of its societies. "Guilt" in this context is a designation with regard to its laws, not to Truth.

When you are truly aware of your eternal innocence you observe the universe of form with detachment. When the personal self is called upon to make a judgment you discern fact from your personal projections so that your judgment is not clouded with guilt. You direct the personal self to play its part in society without judging what it is called upon to do. You rest in peace because you are aware of Truth. You do not confuse yourself with the unfolding story projected from your mind.

6. Judging with an Awareness of Truth instead of Judging with the Personal Thought System

Truth is all that is, so It is the same throughout Itself. Truth has no need for *judgment*, which is evaluative and necessary only in the presence of differences. But not-Truth projects a universe of form with a multitude of different limitations. So judgment is required in the perception that not-Truth is real.

You use judgment in the world in two ways: To make practical decisions and to make form seem real to you. You can make practical decisions with either the personal thought system or your True thought system. But when you use judgment to give reality to form you use only the personal thought system.

a. Using Practical Judgment to Become Aware of Truth

While a personal self is in your awareness you seem to be presented with constant choices and decisions to make for it. This requires judgment. When you are identified with it this is an almost unbearable burden. You believe that the personal self, its story, and its world are real and are all that you have for a limited time. Every decision then carries a significant weight for you. You feel that you must squeeze out of each one as much happiness as is possible for the short time that you have.

And the personal thought system is inherently guilty. Its guilt comes from the belief that it has attacked and undone Truth. So when you identify with it you worry constantly about making the "right" decisions to appease "God", society, your family, and/or some other group or individual to whom you feel responsible.

Also, the personal thought system has no consistent criteria for making decisions. When you are identified with it you are inherently selfish, but what you consider as in your own best interest fluctuates with shifting moods and values. So you are always uncertain about your best course, and you are constantly second-guessing your choices.

But while you still feel that decisions in the world are important they do not have to be about defining and defending an arbitrary, limited identity. Instead they can be the means for you to get in touch with your True thought system and peace. When you call on the Teacher of Truth in your mind to make decisions for the personal self you release yourself from the burden of making decisions with a personal thought system. You release yourself from guilt and fear. When you call on the teacher of Truth and receive an answer you demonstrate that you have not attacked and undone Truth. So practical decisions for the personal self are opportunities for you to choose to experience Truth and to undo guilt. They can be the means to peace rather than ends in themselves.

In time the Truth in your mind will be more real to you than the universe of form. Rather than your mind living through the personal self Truth will live through your mind. Decisions for the personal self will flow from your mind easily and automatically. And you will observe the personal self's life unfolding harmoniously.

b. Releasing Judgment-to-make-not-Truth-real

Beyond the need for practical decisions the personal thought system uses its judgments of right/wrong, good/bad, valuable/valueless to give meaning to the universe of form. This makes it real to you. If you observe the personal thought system you will notice that it is constantly evaluating what it encounters in the world to define and to defend itself. It is through judgment-to-make-real that the personal thought system perpetuates the illusion that the interpretations that it projects onto the universe of form are reality.

One of the personal thought system's judgments is that it is wrong for you to judge others. This judgment is only to reinforce guilt in your mind, not to help you release judgment. So judging others and judging yourself for judging others are both obstacles to peace for you. They do not justify guilt but release.

If you want inner peace you do not want to suppress the personal thought system's judgments-to-make-real. This will only push them away from your conscious awareness, not undo them. You want to let them come up so that you can recognize that they give meaning to nothing. Then you will be able to let them go and be free to turn to the Truth in your mind instead.

The personal thought system will panic at the idea that you do not need its practical judgment or its judgment-to-make-real. It will tell you that the personal self's life in the world will fall apart if you do not follow its guidance. But remember that the personal self is not you. You are the mind thinking about it. When your mind is centered in Truth you are aware that you are whole. This manifests automatically as you knowing how to direct the personal self for its well-being. But the personal thought system is not interested in your well-being, or even in the well-being of the body about which it panics. It is only interested in holding your attention.

Look honestly at what is occurring when you judge with the personal thought system. In the story of form and time and space that it wants you to believe is reality you cannot see everything that has ever happened everywhere in the past or everything that will ever happen everywhere in the future. So you have no real basis for evaluating the little snippet of the story of form and time and space that seems to be unfolding before you now.

Further, the personal thought system is constantly pulled in different directions by conflicting values. Not-Truth has no positive goal. Its entire seeming-purpose is to negate Truth. The personal thought system, then, has no consistent basis for judgment, so its judgments are arbitrary and contradictory.

Every moment the personal thought system seeks only to distract you from Truth with whatever judgments it can conjure up. So look honestly at the personal thought system and when you are tempted to follow its judgment ask yourself if you have any reason to believe that it knows the way to peace.

The Teacher of Truth in your mind uses judgment as long as both Truth and not-Truth seem real to you. It uses practical judgment as a means to gain your awareness and trust. And It uses it to evaluate what is useful for peace in the personal self's life as long as you are still attached to the personal self. Only It can do this because only It can see your way to peace. Ultimately the Teacher of Truth uses judgment to teach you What is True and what is not-True so that you can release the not-True from your mind and be at peace.

All judgment will fall away from your mind when you accept that only the Truth is True and release the personal thought system. Then you will be wholly at peace.

7. Forgiving to Release Not-Truth instead of Forgiving to Validate Not-Truth

Just as with everything else your True thought system and the personal thought system use *forgiving* in diametrically opposed ways. For your True thought system forgiving means letting go of your belief in or attachment to not-Truth and its manifestations. For the personal thought system forgiving is another way of validating not-Truth and guilt as real.

a. Being Forgiven

As was explained in earlier discussions about sin as long as not-Truth is real to you, you believe that you have attacked Truth. Guilt for this seeming-infraction is at the center of every personal thought system. There is no personal thought system without guilt and no guilt in your mind without the personal thought system.

So as long as you identify with a personal self you believe that you need to be forgiven for your "sin" of attacking Truth. *Forgiveness* in this context means release that you seek from something outside of you, often labeled "God". Through the righteous behavior of the personal self you seek to "atone" for your sin. You sacrifice and punish the personal self and its body in the hopes that this will mitigate your god's punishment of you. You fear any good that comes to you because it is undeserved by such a sinner as you. You never know when you have paid enough for your sin. You can only hope that this god outside of you will eventually let you off of the hook.

So when you seek for forgiveness from a god outside of you, you do not undo your identification with a personal self in a body in a world. You hold onto this idea as your reality, reinforcing guilt in your mind.

But Truth is not outside of you. You have not attacked It nor left It. Truth is the constant in your mind, whether you are aware of It or not. Not-Truth in all of its manifestations, including the personal self, is only an erroneous thought in your mind which has no effect on Truth. Your belief in it causes you to think that you do not have peace, and that is all. So *true forgiving* is not something that is done to you but is done by you. It means releasing yourself from your belief in not-True thoughts. Only you can set yourself free because only you hold ideas in your mind that bind you. You forgive your erroneous thoughts for your own peace of mind.

Even in the personal self's relationships in the world it is never another's forgiveness that you really need. If you feel that you have directed the personal self to do something to harm another their forgiveness will mean nothing to you if you do not forgive yourself. This is because it is your own thoughts that cause you pain.

Ultimately what you need to forgive yourself is your identification with a personal self. Specific personal stories of guilt are only manifestations of the guilt that is at the center of the personal identity. But these stories of guilt are what motivate you to turn inward to Truth for relief. When you touch Truth within and remember that It is all that is real the thoughts that you need to release yourself from your belief in your guilt will come to you.

b. Forgiving Others

For a personal self *forgiving another* means releasing them from guilt for something they did or did not do to or for you. The personal thought system directs forgiving outward to reinforce in your mind the idea that others cause your peace or conflict. But what happens in the universe of form has no meaning in itself. So *true forgiving of others* must always be directed toward yourself in the recognition that it is your own thoughts about them that cause your sense of conflict.

As an example, let's say that a friend promised to pick you up to take you to a job interview that you judged as important for the personal self. They didn't show up and you did all that you could to reach them in time. But in the end they simply forgot so you missed the interview. You are now angry with them. You see them as guilty for neglecting your needs. What is making you angry, however, is not that they did not pick you up. Your thoughts about them not picking you up are what anger you: "This was an important interview and they made me miss it", "They are thoughtless, selfish, insensitive", "My life would've been better with this job", "They don't care about me", etc. What you need to forgive, then, is not the person or the situation but your own pain-causing thoughts.

Ultimately true forgiving recognizes that only the Truth is True. It recognizes that there is nothing to forgive because what is not-True is not real. True forgiving always releases you from the pain of believing in not-Truth to the peace of the awareness of Truth. In the above scenario you would overcome your pain-causing thoughts in the recognition that Truth is always untouched within you. You would acknowledge that only your awareness of Truth is the source of your peace. Further, you would know that what shows up in the universe of form is an effect of your mind. If this job was right for you, you would get another chance at it. If it was not right for you something else that is right for you would show up.

True forgiving means that you recognize that only your awareness of Truth is important. However, this does not manifest as the personal self being a door-mat for others. Continuing with the story above you may find yourself moved to sever the friendship with the person who neglected you in a situation that they knew was important to you. Or you may simply modify your friendship with them by recognizing where you can and cannot trust them to be there for you. An awareness of Truth does not lead you to martyrdom. It leads you to accept the limitations of the world and the people in it. You will adjust to this with comfort when you know that the Truth within you is the only constant on which you can rely. This awareness is what leads you to peace.

c. The Results of True Forgiving

True forgiving results in you releasing yourself from your identification with a personal self. You cannot force this. First you must develop your awareness of the Truth as Truth. Then forgiving will come naturally.

When you are aware of Truth you are in a forgiving state of mind. This results in you:

Letting the personal self's feelings and desires be as you rest in peace within.

Letting the personal self's moods be as you rest in peace within.

Letting the personal self go about its business in the world as you rest in peace within.

Letting other personal selves be as you rest in peace within.

Letting the world and its ways and laws be as you rest in peace within.

Apologizing and making amends with ease because you are not attached to the personal self and its self-image.

Accepting apologies and amends with ease because you are not attached to the personal self and its self-image.

Allowing change to occur with an open mind.

Directing the personal self to take action without an attachment to outcome.

Trusting that all is unfolding perfectly in the personal self's story as an effect of your awareness of Truth.

When you are in a forgiving state of mind you do not feel a need to change the personal self in your awareness to make it "right" or "good". You do not feel a need to change others or the world so that you can be at peace. You are honest with yourself about all of the thoughts and feelings passing through your mind. You do not embrace or fight against not-Truth and all of its manifestations. You let them all go.

For example, say at work someone has taken credit for work that you did. This work was important to your position. So this is not only a matter of you not getting credit for a specific project but it makes it look like you are not fulfilling the responsibilities of your position. This threatens your continuing in this particular job. The personal thought system always responds immediately and emotionally. It will attack, certainly the person who took credit for your work and perhaps others and maybe even you. It will rile against its mistreatment. It will see itself as a victim.

When you choose to be forgiving you allow the personal thought system to process out its thoughts and feelings without judgment. You observe it, understanding that all personal selves are inherently guilty, fearful, insecure, and defensive. You let the personal thought system have its say then you let it go as you turn to the Truth within.

When you are aware of the Truth you are not attached to outcomes for the personal self because it is not you. You are at peace and emotionally neutral. In the above scenario when it comes time to go to your superiors with evidence of work done you are able to deal in facts instead of emotions. You lay your side of the story on the table and allow the outcome of your efforts to unfold. You know that whatever the outcome it is the perfect unfolding in form of your awareness of Truth. If there is more action to take, a point to press home, or a fact to highlight, you will know what to do. You will act in confidence, not because you believe that you are "right" or "good", but because you know that the Truth in you is unchanged by anything that does or does not happen in the world.

When you are in a forgiving state of mind you do not take what happens in the world personally. You accept the world as it is in the recognition that it is all just passing thoughts. Only the Truth is True and only the Truth is constant. It is in this awareness that you find release and peace.

8. Openness to Truth instead of Prayer

As the word is generally used *prayer* is a petition toward a higher power outside of you for something that you perceive you lack. In Truth you lack for nothing, so you have no need for prayer. But since not-Truth is a state of lack you could say that as long as you perceive yourself as a limited self in a limited world you are in a state of constant prayer.

a. "Praying for" Yourself

There is nothing outside of you to which you can petition for anything. Truth is within you and It simply is. It does not have power over you. Your experience of peace or conflict comes wholly from your own mind. When you are aware of Truth you are at peace. When you deny Truth you are in conflict.

Truth never has anything to do with the personal self and its story. They are not real. They are just ideas in your mind. But your awareness of Truth manifests as a harmonious personal story unfolding from your mind. You do not have to do anything more than center your mind in Truth for this to happen automatically.

The personal thought system teaches you that peace will come to you from someone or something outside of you. It always imagines a specific form for you to seek to bring you peace. And when one specific form inevitably fails it moves on to seek for peace in another specific form. But lasting peace comes when you are aware of Truth. Truth is universal, not specific. It cannot be contained in a form. The specific forms that show up in the personal self's story when you are aware of Truth do not bring you peace. They manifest the peace in your mind.

You feel lack when you are unaware of your inherent wholeness in Truth. But you do not need to *pray* for anything. You only need to open your mind to Truth. Truth is always present within you. You do not have to petition It to come into your awareness. Your obstacles to It are in your mind. You only have to let go of your obstacles to Truth and It will be in your awareness.

Truth does not need your words to come into your awareness. But you may use words to quiet your mind, to center it in Truth, to speak with the Teacher of Truth, to remind yourself that Truth is right here, and to express to yourself your willingness to have Truth in your awareness. More important than words, however, is a feeling of true openness to Truth. Your willingness, not your words, is the way to inner peace.

b. "Praying for" Others

Praying for others is the same as praying for yourself. There is no power over you or over what you perceive to petition for help. If you want peace you only need to open your mind to Truth.

If something in the universe of form disturbs you it does not matter whether it seems to be happening to the personal self in your awareness or to another. Your being disturbed is caused by thoughts in your mind, not by what is appearing. So you only need to attend to your own mind.

For example, say a friend has asked you to pray for her while she undergoes treatment for cancer. You tell her that you will because you know that this comforts her. But within yourself you know that there is nothing about which to pray and nothing to which to pray. You know that the story unfolding before you is not Truth. It is a passing idea. Sometimes it is a happy story; sometimes it is a sad story. But you are not attached to its pleasures or tortured by its pains because you know that it all passes. Truth is the only constant.

However, if you find yourself more than just temporarily saddened and you are unable to stay centered in Truth then you have to look with the Teacher of Truth in your mind at the thoughts that are your obstacles to peace. Maybe her illness brings up unresolved grief from the past. It may bring up your own fears of illness or mortality. Perhaps you are so attached to your friend that you think that you cannot live without her. Or you may feel helpless and wish that you could comfort her by telling her that the Truth is within her. If you are not sure why you cannot simply let this situation unfold as it will then ask the Teacher of Truth in your mind to help you find the thoughts in your way so that you can release them and return to peace.

9. The Unity of Truth instead of Personal Joining

The unity of Truth is the all-encompassing nature of Truth. Truth is all that is. It is everywhere always. In Truth there is only Truth and It is all the same throughout Itself. So the unity of Truth is by definition formless, infinite, and eternal (timeless).When you experience the unity of Truth you experience wholeness. It is an experience of never-ending love and peace and joy.

Because your mind is naturally unified in your belief that it is split between Truth and not-Truth you are compelled to seek for unity. You do this by trying to "spiritualize" not-Truth. This means that you try to give to not-Truth the attributes of Truth, which has been discussed earlier. But you also seek for unity through the personal self where you will never find it.

Not-Truth is the opposite of Truth. Its universe of form is finite, time-bound, and diverse. It is not unified. So in your identification with a personal self you long for unity. To address this longing the personal thought system makes its own form of "oneness". But this is not any type of unity. It is actually a validation of the reality of not-Truth.

The form of oneness that it uses to replace True unity is to bring the personal self's body into proximity with other bodies with a common interest. Sometimes this is with one other body. Sometimes this is with a small or large group of bodies. But the longing for unity in your mind is real and it is not satisfied by the joining of limited forms that are only effects of your mind. This is why you are still lonely when you are with other personal selves. And this is why personal relationships in the world are so conflicted. Each looks to the other or others for the experience of wholeness that another cannot give. When you realize this in one relationship the personal thought system will blame the other personal self or selves. It will tell you to seek for wholeness with the "right" body or bodies. The personal thought system is quite content with you seeking for wholeness through the personal self because you will never find it

Only in the Truth within you can you find the wholeness for which you long. When you no longer look to the personal self's relationship to supply the wholeness that they never can supply they become manifestations of your awareness of your wholeness instead. They unfold harmoniously as the personal self relates to others from wholeness rather than from lack.

In its desire for unity the split mind will not only seek for it on the level of seemingly-individual minds. In more general terms it will project a type of oneness into its story for the universe of form. This is manifested as seeing unity in the universe of form, often expressed through its sciences. For example, geneticists note that all human beings are descended from one individual who lived in Africa millennia ago. Physics has come to "discover" that there is a single energy or force behind all matter. Atoms from the beginning of the universe of form are all still around and make up all form, even bodies. These concepts may be metaphors for oneness, but they are not the unity of Truth. Energy and forces are forms, though unseen. All form is not-True.

You can find and experience the unity of Truth only within you. When you long for wholeness turn inward. The Truth is the oneness that you are truly seeking. Only in It will you find lasting peace.

a. True Love instead of Personal Love

In Truth *love* is the experience of the unity of Truth. But for the personal thought system *love* has a meaning other than oneness and wholeness. It may speak in terms of "two becoming one" through their love and it teaches you to seek for another to make you whole. But its goal is to keep you unaware of True love and actual wholeness.

The personal thought system's chief distraction to keep you from the True love within you is the personal-love relationship in its many forms. True love is impersonal because the Truth within you is universal. Universality is what oneness means. But the personal thought system sees each personal-love relationship as unique. It uses them to validate the personal self as your identity. You and another, whether lover, spouse, child, parent, sibling, or friend, "love" each other because of a given relationship, for what you can get from each other, and/or for the role or roles that you play with each other.

Your desire for personal love leads outward to attachment to form (bodies, personalities, roles, situations) in the belief that form supplies love. Your awareness of True love within results in detachment from form in the recognition that form is meaningless. Personal love has boundaries, limitations, and conditions. True love is limitless. Personal love is directed toward an object of love. True love simply is, always and everywhere. Personal love leads to you directing the personal self to act for your emotional satisfaction, either from the action itself or in return from the loved one. True love manifests as the personal self behaving lovingly as the natural effect of your mind knowing that it is love.

As you become aware of the Truth within you and you detach from form the personal thought system will accuse you of becoming "cold" and "uncaring". But you will not experience the love within you as cold. Nor will others experience you as uncaring. On the contrary, they will find you loving. That is unless they "loved" you only on condition that you played a certain role in their drama. As you grow more aware of the love within you forms of un-lovingness will fall away from your awareness. You will find the personal self surrounded by loving relationships that manifest the love within you.

b. Awareness of Truth and Healthy Boundaries

One way that the personal thought system seeks to fulfill your longing for True unity through the personal self's relationships is by dropping the boundaries between the personal self and others. This means that you take responsibility for the thoughts, feelings, and actions of other personal selves. You enable them to remain immature, dysfunctional, or in an active disease, like addiction or mental illness. Or you ask others to take responsibility for your thoughts, feelings, and actions to enable you to remain immature, dysfunctional, or in an active disease. The result is that the one who takes on more responsibility becomes a martyr. They feel burdened and resentful and victimized in the relationship. And the one who gives up more responsibility feels manipulated, constrained, and also victimized.

The personal thought system calls this co-dependency "caring" or "loving". That's because the personal thought system associates love with sacrifice, its highest value. So by extension it equates love with resentment and pain. This belief reinforces fear of love in your mind. Your fear of personal love extends to fear of True love and functions as an obstacle to peace for you.

The personal thought system says, "You lack; let me fix you" or "I lack; let me fix you" or "I lack; you fix me". But your True thought system says, "Only the Truth is True and I am whole in Truth." It does not believe in personal selves and their stories, which are ideas of limitation and lack. This manifests in your awareness as a healthy, whole personal self with appropriate boundaries with others.

Other healthy personal selves accept boundaries with gratitude. They recognize them as acknowledgement of their wholeness. But unhealthy personal selves find boundaries baffling or cold or hard. Those who prefer drama and pain will fall away when you no longer enable them or want to be enabled by them. But whatever others' response to your boundaries you will be at peace. The personal story that manifests in your awareness will harmoniously reflect this.

10. Learning From the Teacher of Truth instead of Learning From Others

It is the Law of Mind that mind knows only itself. In Truth this means that Truth knows only Truth. Truth is complete, so in Truth there is nothing to learn. But in not-Truth, which is nothing, you cannot know anything. So you must learn instead. And since all that you are really lacking is the awareness of what you are all that you must learn is what you are. "What am I?" is the only real question in your split mind. The not-True thought system in your mind teaches you to reinforce your identification with a personal self. Your True thought system teaches you to remind you that Truth is all that there is.

The facts that you seem to learn in the world about the universe of form and its stories are not real lessons. They are affirmations of not-Truth. When you seem to be learning about the universe of form you are not really learning because there is nothing there to learn. Your only real lessons are what the Teacher of Truth in your mind has to teach you. This is because It teaches you the Truth. Since only the Truth is real you can only really learn of the Truth.

Since your mind can only know itself then every moment you teach yourself what you believe you are by the thought system in your mind that you choose to follow. So you only ever teach yourself and you only ever learn from yourself. Every moment you reinforce in your mind the reality of the thought system that you choose to follow.

This is true for every seemingly-individual mind. And this is why a single spiritual teaching is heard or read in different ways by seemingly-different minds. The speaker or writer learns from the thought system from which they teach. But what others hear or read depends on the thought system that they choose within their own minds. If they are centered in Truth they will hear from Truth what they are ready to learn from Truth. If they are centered in the personal thought system they will hear something that frightens them.

You may feel guided or compelled to direct the personal self to teach the Truth to seeming-others in the world through speaking and/or writing. What you strongly desire to teach is what you strongly desire to learn. Your mind inherently understands that what it teaches it reinforces in itself.

If you are truly guided to teach by the Teacher of Truth you will begin to teach others when you are ready to learn how to put aside the personal thought system and teach from the Truth within you. You will teach from experience and this will be your way of learning that you are Truth.

If instead you are compelled to teach by the personal thought system in your mind your teaching will reinforce the personal self as your identity. The personal thought system is more than happy to commandeer the concept of Truth for its own glorification. When you teach from the personal thought system you can only teach from theory because in the personal thought system you cannot experience Truth. To not-Truth Truth is not true. It is just a nice idea that it can use for its own ends.

You will know that you are teaching from Truth when what you teach leads you to a joyful sense of liberation from limitations. You will not be concerned with the form and outcome of your teaching, which are only effects of your awareness of Truth. You will understand that your awareness of Truth is all that matters for inner peace.

You will be grateful that teaching reinforces Truth in your awareness. So you will be happy to make the personal self available to others if they seek teaching from you. But you will feel no need to teach to change others. You will know that you only have to change your own mind to be at peace. You will recognize that what others learn from you is determined by the thought system that they choose to follow, not by you. In other words, teaching will not be personal for you. It will be the natural manifestation of your awareness of Truth.

But if you teach from the personal thought system you will continue to feel bound to limitations. You will have an attachment to how your words are read or heard because your goal for teaching will be to be seen as "right". You will be driven by a need to help or to fix others or the world because you will still be projecting your conflict onto them. Being a spiritual teacher will be important to your self-concept and you will be attached to this role. When you teach from the personal thought system teaching is personal for you.

As a student you do not have to be concerned with spiritual teachers but rather with their teaching. The Teacher of Truth within you is your only real teacher. With any teaching, written or spoken, the Teacher of Truth will help you to sort out Truth from not-Truth. If a teaching is in line with Truth the Teacher of Truth will reinforce it. If a teaching is not in line with Truth the Teacher of Truth will use its contrast with Truth to teach you about Truth. When you study for inner peace with the Teacher of Truth you never have to fear that you will be misled. You can rest in peace knowing that you will be led to Truth.

About the Author

Liz Cronkhite is a mentor for students of *A Course in Miracles* and *4 Habits for Inner Peace*, has written hundreds of articles clarifying the *Course* for other students, and is the translator of *The Plain Language A Course in Miracles*. You can learn more about her and what she offers at www.4habitsforinnerpeace.com.

Printed in Great Britain
by Amazon.co.uk, Ltd.,
Marston Gate.